MACMILLAN MASTER GUIDES

GENERAL EDITOR: JAMES GIBSON

Published

MACMILLAN MASTER GUIDES

THOMAS MIDDLETON and WILLIAM ROWLEY	*The Changeling* Tony Bromham
ARTHUR MILLER	*The Crucible* Leonard Smith *Death of a Salesman* Peter Spalding
GEORGE ORWELL	*Animal Farm* Jean Armstrong
WILLIAM SHAKESPEARE	*Richard II* Charles Barber *Hamlet* Jean Brooks *King Lear* Francis Casey *Henry V* Peter Davison *The Winter's Tale* Diana Devlin *Julius Caesar* David Elloway *Macbeth* David Elloway *Measure for Measure* Mark Lilly *Henry IV Part I* Helen Morris *Romeo and Juliet* Helen Morris *The Tempest* Kenneth Pickering *A Midsummer Night's Dream* Kenneth Pickering *Coriolanus* Gordon Williams *Antony and Cleopatra* Martin Wine
GEORGE BERNARD SHAW	*St Joan* Leonée Ormond
RICHARD SHERIDAN	*The School for Scandal* Paul Ranger *The Rivals* Jeremy Rowe
ALFRED TENNYSON	*In Memoriam* Richard Gill
ANTHONY TROLLOPE	*Barchester Towers* K. M. Newton
JOHN WEBSTER	*The White Devil* and *The Duchess of Malfi* David A. Male
VIRGINIA WOOLF	*To the Lighthouse* John Mepham *Mrs Dalloway* Julian Pattison

Forthcoming

CHARLOTTE BRONTË	*Jane Eyre* Robert Miles
JOHN BUNYAN	*The Pilgrim's Progress* Beatrice Batson
T. S. ELIOT	*Murder in the Cathedral* Paul Lapworth *Selected Poems* Andrew Swarbrick
BEN JONSON	*Volpone* Michael Stout
RUDYARD KIPLING	*Kim* Leonée Ormond
JOHN MILTON	*Comus* Tom Healy
WILLIAM SHAKESPEARE	*Othello* Tony Bromham *As You Like It* Kiernan Ryan
VIRGINIA WOOLF	*Mrs Dalloway* Julian Pattison
W. B. YEATS	*Selected Poems* Stan Smith

MACMILLAN MASTER GUIDES
ANTONY AND CLEOPATRA
BY WILLIAM SHAKESPEARE

MARTIN WINE

with an Introduction by
HAROLD BROOKS

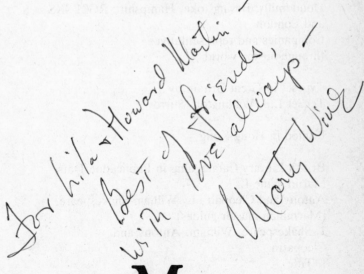

For Lila & Howard Martin
Best of friends,
with love always,
Marty Wine

M
MACMILLAN
EDUCATION

First edition 1987

Published by
MACMILLAN EDUCATION LTD
Houndmills, Basingstoke, Hampshire RG21 2XS
and London
Companies and representatives
throughout the world

Typeset in Great Britain by
TecSet Ltd, Wallington, Surrey

Printed in Hong Kong

British Library Cataloguing in Publication Data
Martin Wine L.
Antony and Cleopatra by William Shakespeare.
(Macmillan master guides)
1. Shakespeare, William. Antony and
Cleopatra
I. Title
822.3'3   PR2802
ISBN 0–333–42784–X Pbk
ISBN 0–333–42786–9 Pbk export

CONTENTS

GENERAL EDITOR'S PREFACE

The aim of the Macmillan Master Guides is to help you to appreciate the book you are studying by providing information about it and by suggesting ways of reading and thinking about it which will lead to a fuller understanding. The section on the writer's life and background has been designed to illustrate those aspects of the writer's life which have influenced the work, and to place it in its personal and literary context. The summaries and critical commentary are of special importance in that each brief summary of the action is followed by an examination of the significant critical points. The space which might have been given to repetitive explanatory notes has been devoted to a detailed analysis of the kind of passage which might confront you in an examination. Literary criticism is concerned with both the broader aspects of the work being studied and with its detail. The ideas which meet us in reading a great work of literature, and their relevance to us today, are an essential part of our study, and our Guides look at the thought of their subject in some detail. But just as essential is the craft with which the writer has constructed his work of art, and this may be considered under several technical headings – characterisation, language, style and stagecraft, for example.

The authors of these Guides are all teachers and writers of wide experience, and they have chosen to write about books they admire and know well in the belief that they can communicate their admiration to you. But you yourself must read and know intimately the book you are studying. No one can do that for you. You should see this book as a lamp-post. Use it to shed light, not to lean against. If you know your text and know what it is saying about life, and how it says it, then you will enjoy it, and there is no better way of passing an examination in literature.

JAMES GIBSON

AN INTRODUCTION TO THE STUDY OF SHAKESPEARE'S PLAYS

A play as a work of art exists to the full only when performed. It must hold the audience's attention throughout the performance, and, unlike a novel, it can't be put down and taken up again. It is important to experience the play as if you are seeing it on the stage for the first time, and you should begin by reading it straight through. Shakespeare builds a play in dramatic units which may be divided into smaller subdivisions, or episodes, marked off by exits and entrances and lasting as long as the same actors are on the stage. Study it unit by unit.

The first unit provides the exposition which is designed to put the audience into the picture. In the second unit we see the forward movement of the play as one situation changes into another. The last unit in a tragedy or a tragical play will bring the catastrophe, and in comedy – and some of the history plays – an unravelling of the complications, what is called a *dénouement*.

The onward movement of the play from start to finish is its progressive structure. We see the chain of cause and effect (the plot) and the progressive revelation and development of character. The people, their characters and their motives drive the plot forward in a series of scenes which are carefully planned to give variety of pace and excitement. We notice fast-moving and slower-moving episodes, tension mounting and slackening, and alternative fear and hope for the characters we favour. Full-stage scenes, such as stately councils and processions or turbulent mobs, contrast with scenes of small groups or even single speakers. Each of the scenes presents a deed or event which changes the situation. In performances, entrances and exits and stage actions are physical facts, with more impact than on the page. That impact Shakespeare relied upon, and we must restore it by an effort of the imagination.

Shakespeare's language is just as diverse. Quickfire dialogue is followed by long speeches, and verse changes to prose. There is a wide range of speech — formal, colloquial, dialect, 'Mummerset' and the broken English of foreigners, for example. Songs, instrumental music, and the noise of battle, revelry and tempest, all extend the range of dramatic expression. The dramatic use of language is enhanced by skilful stagecraft, by costumes, by properties such as beds, swords and Yorick's skull, by such stage business as kneeling, embracing and giving money, and by use of such features of the stage structure as the balcony and the trapdoor.

By these means Shakespeare's people are brought vividly to life and cleverly individualised. But though they have much to tell us about human nature, we must never forget that they are characters in a play, not in real life. And remember, they exist to enact the play, not the play to portray *them*.

Shakespeare groups his characters so that they form a pattern, and it is useful to draw a diagram showing this. Sometimes a linking character has dealings with each group. The pattern of persons belongs to the symmetric structure of the play, and its dramatic unity is reinforced and enriched by a pattern of resemblances and contrasts; for instance, between characters, scenes, recurrent kinds of imagery, and words. It is not enough just to notice a feature that belongs to the symmetric structure, you should ask what its relevance is to the play as a whole and to the play's ideas.

These ideas and the dramatising of them in a central theme, or several related to each other, are a principal source of the dramatic unity. In order to see what themes are present and important, look, as before, for pattern. Observe the place in it of the leading character. In tragedy this will be the protagonist, in comedy heroes and heroines, together with those in conflict or contrast with them. In *Henry IV Part I,* Prince Hal is being educated for kingship and has a correct estimate of honour, while Falstaff despises honour, and Hotspur makes an idol of it. Pick out the episodes of great intensity as, for example, in *King Lear* where the theme of spiritual blindness is objectified in the blinding of Gloucester, and similarly, note the emphases given by dramatic poetry as in Prospero's 'Our revels now are ended . . .'or unforgettable utterances such as Lear's 'Is there any cause in Nature that makes these hard hearts?' Striking stage-pictures such as that of Hamlet behind the King at prayer will point to leading themes, as will all the parallels and recurrences, including those of phrase and imagery. See whether, in the play you are studying, themes known to be favourites with Shakespeare are prominent, themes such as those of order and dis-order, relationships disrupted by mistakes about identity, and appearance and reality. The latter were bound to fascinate Shakespeare, whose theatrical art worked by means of illusions which pointed beyond the surface of actual life to underlying truths. In looking at themes beware of attempts to make the play fit some orthodoxy a critic believes in − Freudian perhaps, or Marxist, or dogmatic Christian theology − and remember that its ideas, though they often have a bearing on ours, are Elizabethan.

Some of Shakespeare's greatness lies in the good parts he wrote for the actors. In his demands upon them, and the opportunities he provided, he bore their professional skills in mind and made use of their physical prowess, relished by a public accustomed to judge fencing and wrestling as expertly as we today judge football and tennis. As a member of the professional group of players called the Chamberlain's Men he knew each actor he was writing for. To play his women he had highly trained boys. As paired heroines they were often contrasted, short with tall, for example, or one vivacious and enterprising, the other more conventionally feminine.

Richard Burbage, the company's leading man, was famous as a great tragic actor, and he took leading roles in seven of Shakespeare's *tragedies*. Though each of the seven has its own distinctiveness, we shall find at the centre of all of them a tragic protagonist possessing tragic greatness, not just one 'tragic flaw' but a tragic vulnerability. He will have a character which makes him unfit to cope with the tragic situations confronting him, so that his tragic errors bring down upon him tragic suffering and finally a tragic catastrophe. Normally, both the suffering and the catastrophe are far worse than he can be said to deserve, and others are engulfed in them who deserve such a fate less or not at all. Tragic terror is aroused in us because, though exceptional, he is sufficiently near to normal humankind for his fate to remind us of what can happen to human beings like ourselves, and because we see in it a combination of inexorable law and painful mystery. We recognise the principle of cause and effect where in a tragic world errors return upon those who make them, but we are also aware of the tragic disproportion between cause and effect. In a tragic world you may kick a stone and start an avalanche which will destroy you and others with you. Tragic pity is aroused in us by this disproportionate suffering, and also by all the kinds of suffering undergone by every character who has won our imaginative sympathy. Imaginative sympathy is wider than moral approval, and is felt even if suffering does seem a just and logical outcome. In addition to pity and terror we have a sense of tragic waste because catastrophe has affected so much that was great and fine. Yet we feel also a tragic exaltation. To our grief the men and women who represented those values have been destroyed, but the values themselves have been shown not to depend upon success, nor upon immunity from the worst of tragic sufferings and disaster.

Comedies have been of two main kinds, or cross-bred from the two. In critical comedies the governing aim is to bring out the absurdity or irrationality of follies and abuses, and make us laugh at them. Shakespeare's comedies often do this, but most of them belong primarily to the other kind – romantic comedy. Part of the romantic appeal is to our liking for suspense; they are dramas of averted threat, beginning in trouble and ending in joy. They appeal to the romantic senses of adventure and of wonder, and to complain that they are improbable is silly because the improbability, the marvellousness, is part of the pleasure. They dramatise stories of romantic love, accompanied by love doctrine – ideas and ideals of love. But they are plays in two tones, they are comic as well as romantic. There is often something to laugh at even in the love stories of the nobility and gentry, and just as there is high comedy in such incidents as the cross-purposes of the young Athenians in the wood, and Rosalind as 'Ganymede' teasing Orlando, there is always broad comedy for characters of lower rank. Even where one of the sub-plots has no effect on the main plot, it may take up a topic from it and present it in a more comic way.

What is there in the play to make us laugh or smile? We can distinguish many kinds of comedy it may employ. *Language* can amuse by its wit, or by absurdity, as in Bottom's malapropisms. Feste's nonsense-phrases, so fatuously admired by Sir Andrew, are deliberate, while his catechising of Olivia is clown-routine. Ass-headed Bottom embraced by the Fairy Queen is a *comic spectacle* combining costume and stage-business. His wanting to play every part is *comedy of character*. Phebe disdaining Silvius and in love with 'Ganymede', or Malvolio treating Olivia as though she had written him a love-letter is *comedy of situation*; the situation is laughably different from what Phebe or Malvolio supposes. A comic let-down or anticlimax can be devastating, as we see when Aragon, sure that he deserves Portia, chooses the silver casket only to find the portrait not of her but of a 'blinking idiot'. By *slapstick, caricature* or sheer *ridiculousness of situation*, comedy can be exaggerated into farce, which Shakespeare knows how to use on occasion. At the opposite extreme, before he averts the threat, he can carry it to the brink of tragedy, but always under control.

Dramatic irony is the result of a character or the audience anticipating an outcome which, comically or tragically, turns out very differently. Sometimes *we* foresee that it will. The speaker never foresees how ironical, looking back, the words or expectations will appear. When she says, 'A little water clears us of this deed,' Lady Macbeth has no prevision of her sleep-walking words, 'Will these hands ne'er be clean?' There is irony in the way in which in all Shakespeare's tragic plays except *Richard II* comedy is found in the very heart of the tragedy. The Porter scene in *Macbeth* comes straight after Duncan's murder. In *Hamlet* and *Antony and Cleopatra* comic episodes lead into the catastrophe: the rustic Countryman brings Cleopatra the means of death, and the satirised Osric departs with Hamlet's assent to the fatal fencing match. The Porter, the Countryman and Osric are not mere 'comic relief', they contrast with the tragedy in a way that adds something to it, and affects our response.

A sense of the comic and the tragic is common ground between Shakespeare and his audience. Understandings shared with the audience are necessary to all drama. They include conventions, i.e. assumptions, contrary to what factual realism would demand, which the audience silently agrees to accept. It is, after all, by a convention, what Coleridge called a 'willing suspension of disbelief', that an actor is accepted as Hamlet. We should let a play teach us the conventions it depends on. Shakespeare's conventions allow him to take a good many liberties, and he never troubles about inconsistencies that wouldn't trouble an audience. What matters to the dramatist is the effect he creates. So long as we are responding as he would wish, Shakespeare would not care whether we could say by what means he has made us do so. But to appreciate his skill, and get a fuller understanding of his play, we have to distinguish these means, and find terms to describe them.

If you approach the Shakespeare play you are studying bearing in mind what is said to you here, then you will respond to it more fully than before. Yet like all works of artistic genius, Shakespeare's can only be analysed so far. His drama and its poetry will always have about them something 'which into words no critic can digest'.

HAROLD BROOKS

ACKNOWLEDGEMENTS

All quotations are from *Antony and Cleopatra*, edited by Jan McKeith and Richard Adams (Macmillan Education, 1984). Scenes with pros will cause line numbering to vary among editions; but, since references are clearly identified, this Study Guide may be used with any edition of the play.

Special thanks to colleagues and students: Allan Casson, Jeffrey Collord, Barbara Eaton, John Curtis Johnson, Moody Prior and Sharon Sloan.

Cover illustration: a detail from the sketch of *The Meeting of Antony and Cleopatra* by G. B. Tiepolo. The drawing of the Globe Theatre is by courtesy of Alec Pearson.

1 LIFE AND BACKGROUND

1.1 LIFE

'He was not of an age, but for all time!' The verdict of posterity justifies Ben Jonson's famous praise of his fellow playwright. So much is Shakespeare 'for all time', however, that many people find difficulty in believing that our greatest drama, as well as our greatest poetry, was written by the eldest son of a 'mere' Warwickshire glove-maker and leather-dresser; but the facts of Shakespeare's life are sufficiently documented, beginning with his baptism in Holy Trinity Church in Stratford-upon-Avon on 26 April 1564. The actual date of his birth is open to quesion, but there is no harm in accepting the traditional date of 23 April since infants at this time customarily were baptised three days after birth. The date also coincides, conveniently, with the known day of Shakespeare's death. It is a happy coincidence, too, that on this day England celebrates the day of its patron saint, St George.

Of Shakespeare's early years we know nothing. As the son of a prominent Stratford burgess, who was for a while the town's Bailiff (or Mayor, as we would say today), he almost certainly attended the local grammar school where he would have been given a substantial grounding in classical literature and rhetoric. By the age of twenty-one, he was already a married man with three children. A licence, dated 27 November 1582, for his marriage to Anne Hathaway, eight years his senior, and the baptism of their daughter Susanna in Holy Trinity Church on 26 May 1583 have given rise to speculation of a hasty or forced marriage; but Elizabethan custom did make betrothal legally binding and, under certain circumstances, even permitted 'conjugal rights' – one of the plot devices in Shakespeare's *Measure for Measure* hinges on this custom. On 2 February 1585 the Shakespeare twins, Hamnet and Judith, were christened.

The years 1585 – 92 are frequently referred to as 'the lost years' since no documentation exists for them. An attractive speculation is that, as his father's fortunes declined, the young Shakespeare decided to make his living away from Stratford and joined one of the acting companies that frequented the area. At any rate, we know that by 1592 he was attracting sufficient attention to cause one of the so-called 'University Wits', a fellow playwright, Robert Greene, to mock this 'upstart crow'. Greene had reason to be jealous, for the public record from this point until the end of Shakespeare's life highlights a success story unmatched by any of his contemporaries in the theatrical world. (The private record is marred by the death of his son Hamnet in 1596.) In 1598, a Cambridge graduate, Francis Meres, cited Shakespeare as 'most excellent' for both his comedies and tragedies, twelve of which he named. Earlier, in 1593 and in 1594, Shakespeare published two narrative poems, *Venus and Adonis* and *The Rape of Lucrece*, with dedications to the Earl of Southampton; but the dramatist clearly did not earn his livelihood by means of aristocratic patronage. In 1594 he joined the Lord Chamberlain's company when it was first organized, and to that troupe (after 1603 the King's Men) he remained loyal throughout his professional life. The 'infinite variety' that is ascribed to Cleopatra in *Antony and Cleopatra* (II.ii.237) is an apt description of Shakespeare's own later life as a major actor and the leading dramatist and part-owner of the premier acting company of his day, as well as a wealthy property owner in both Stratford and London.

Shakespeare's last years were spent in Stratford, with occasional visits to London on legal matters and, possibly, to 'doctor' some plays for his company. A monument near his grave informs us that he died on 23 April 1616; he was buried two days later in Stratford's Holy Trinity Church. In 1623, two of his fellow actors and shareholders, John Heminge and Henry Condell, published a collection of thirty-six of his plays, many, like *Antony and Cleopatra*, seeing print for the first time. This was the First Folio, for which Ben Jonson wrote his magnificent tribute.

1.2 'ANTONY AND CLEOPATRA' IN THE CONTEXT OF THE LATER PLAYS

The order in which Shakespeare wrote his plays is by no means certain, but there is general agreement that *Antony and Cleopatra* follows *Macbeth*, the last of the so-called 'four great tragedies' that also include *Hamlet*, *Othello*, and *King Lear*. These plays raise profound questions about the purpose of human existence and the nature of good and evil in an atmosphere of the greatest tragic intensity. But *Antony and Cleopatra* seems to represent a lessening of tragic intensity and a foreshadowing of the final plays — the sequence of 'dramatic romances' that begins with *Pericles* and goes on through *Cymbeline, The Winter's Tale*, and *The Tempest*. In these plays humanity is given a second chance: love, forgiveness, repentance and reconciliation make possible the triumph of life over death.

Although death is not a necessary component of tragedy as an art form, Shakespeare's tragic heroes all meet with death; but the deaths of Antony and Cleopatra do not seem to be accompanied by the same kind of metaphysical horror or bleakness or resignation that we associate with those of the other tragic figures. Death seems almost joyful in *Antony and Cleopatra*. It brings together Antony's public and private selves and restores him to complete humanity; and it justifies his faith in Cleopatra, whose death is so splendid a ritual that it makes the life of the successful Caesars of 'our dungy earth' seem 'paltry' in comparison. There is a transcendent quality to their deaths, in part owing to poetry of uplifting grandeur. In the first scene, Cleopatra teases Antony with the idea of setting a 'bourn' or boundary to their love, but his magnificent reply is that their love cannot be contained by any boundaries of this world. Only a 'new heaven, new earth' can do that. Their deaths give them that boundless eternity of love and simultaneously immortalize them among the greatest lovers of all time. To find that transcendent life, however, they first had to die. As Cleopatra says, 'but woe, 'tis so!' In the final plays, that 'new heaven, new earth' becomes a possibility, even if only temporarily, in this life. For that reason, *Antony and Cleopatra* marks a transition from Shakespeare's earlier tragedies to his later romances.

1.3 'JULIUS CAESAR' AND 'ANTONY AND CLEOPATRA'

Scholars date *Antony and Cleopatra* around 1606–7 and *Julius Caesar* around 1599. The inspiration for both plays was Sir Thomas North's 1579 translation of Plutarch's *Lives of Noble Grecians and Romans* from the French of Jacques Amyot. The earlier play shows Mark Antony and the young Octavius Caesar joining forces to avenge the assassination of Julius Caesar in 44 B.C.; it ends with the deaths of the two leading conspirators, Brutus and Cassius, at Philippi in 42 B.C. The later play begins in 40 B.C. with Antony, young Caesar and Lepidus established as Rome's Triumvirate, and with Antony living at the court of Cleopatra in Alexandria; it ends in 30 B.C. with the deaths of Antony and Cleopatra and the triumph of Octavius Caesar as sole emperor of the Roman world. Whether Shakespeare had in mind a sequel to *Julius Caesar* as he was writing it is unknown, but its conclusion hints at the impending rivalry between Mark Antony and Octavius Caesar and the eventual fall of Antony. Octavius — almost twenty years younger than Antony – is Julius Caesar's nephew, adopted by his uncle as son and heir. In some respects, Antony, the older soldier, is mentor to Octavius; but the pupil makes it clear that he has a will of his own and is just marking time until he can boldly assert himself.

In *Julius Caesar* Cassius refers to Antony as 'a masker and a reveller'. At the beginning of *Antony and Cleopatra*, the Romans apparently have had this view confirmed by Antony's lengthy sojourn at the luxurious court of Cleopatra. Only one Roman in either play intuitively and truly understands the deeper qualities of Antony, and that is Julius Caesar himself. Comparing him to Cassius, Caesar says, 'He loves no plays / As thou dost, Antony; he hears no music'. To the great Caesar, Antony, aware of the pleasure and the beauty that this world offers, is a man with a rich and full inner life and, for that reason, to be trusted. And Caesar's good opinion of Antony is confirmed by Antony's loyalty to his memory after the assassination. Personal relationships always come first for Antony. The animating force behind the second half of *Julius Caesar* is Antony's unswerving desire to revenge his friend and patron and to restore his good name. That achieved, Antony retires to Egypt and to a life of pleasure, as we see at the beginning of *Antony and Cleopatra*. Although only two years have passed since Philippi, the later play shows us an Antony keenly aware of his ageing and, perhaps, beginning to weary of world affairs. He is resolute, it is true, in answering Rome's call to return and save the Triumvirate from the threat of Sextus Pompeius; but we sense in him a growing conviction that there is more to life than the struggle for political power. This later Antony is out of tune with the new order of the younger Caesar and his ambitious followers; spiritually, he belongs in the more heroic and more humane world of Julius Caesar.

2 SUMMARIES AND CRITICAL COMMENTARY

2.1 SUMMARY OF THE PLAY

At the end of *Julius Caesar*, Mark Antony, Octavius Caesar, and
Marcus Æmilius Lepidus assume the triple rule of the Roman Empire
after the assassination of Julius Caesar. *Antony and Cleopatra* begins
with Antony in Egypt, where he has fallen in love with the queen,
Cleopatra, and is neglecting his duties back in Rome. His wife Fulvia
has been waging war against Caesar as a ruse to bring her husband
home; Sextus Pompeius, the son of Pompey the Great, is threatening
Rome in Antony's absence; and Antony's own soldiers are demoral-
ized by what they consider their general's 'dotage'. News of Fulvia's
death is the spur that Antony needs to prompt his return to Rome – a
return that surprises both Caesar and Pompey. To cement a new
bond of friendship with his younger rival, Antony agrees to marry
Caesar's newly-widowed sister Octavia. Now the Triumvirate can
present a united front against Pompey, with whom a treaty is signed.
A soothsayer convinces Antony that Caesar's 'fortunes shall rise
higher' than his own; and Antony's own thoughts turn back to the
East, where his 'pleasure lies'.

Later, established in Athens with Octavia, Antony hears that
Caesar has renewed the war against Pompey without informing him
and, even worse, that he has imprisoned Lepidus and sentenced him
to death. Octavia leaves for Rome to mediate with her brother; but,
in the meantime, Antony returns to Cleopatra, thereby giving Caesar
the excuse that he has needed all along to declare war against the one
remaining triumvir and to become sole emperor. Cleopatra insists on
being an active participant in the war and even encourages Antony to
fight Caesar at sea against the advice of his soldiers who know that he
has the advantage on land. During the ensuing battle, however,
Cleopatra flees from the scene and Antony suffers a humiliating loss
by immediately following after her. Caesar refuses Antony's terms
for peace but, instead, sends an ambassador, Thidias, to Cleopatra to

assure her of 'gentle' treatment if she banishes Antony from Egypt or has him killed. Seeing Cleopatra offer Thidias her hand to be kissed, Antony loses control of himself and orders Caesar's ambassador to be whipped. Enobarbus, Antony's trusted adviser and confidant, now joins others who have deserted Antony; later, he regrets his decision and dies broken-hearted. In the meantime, war breaks out again, and Antony has a short-lived victory fighting Caesar's forces on land; but in a final battle – at sea again, only because Caesar has dared him – Antony sees that all is lost when his own fleet surrenders to Caesar; he is convinced that Cleopatra has betrayed him. He is about to commit suicide when Cleopatra, trying to appease him, has word sent to him that she is dead; he now looks upon death as the means of restoring him to both honour and Cleopatra.

Antony's servant Eros takes his own life rather than help his master to commit suicide, and Antony's own attempt is a botched affair. Cleopatra, fearing that Antony might take his life, now sends word that she is indeed alive. Antony asks to be taken to her monument, where she has hidden to be secure from Caesar, and there he dies in her arms. Left alone, Cleopatra negotiates with Caesar and his ambassadors; but she is merely buying time to outwit her conqueror and thus deny him the glory of leading her in triumph in Rome. As a tribute to Antony, she commits suicide 'after the high Roman fashion'; and even Caesar is impressed by her last act of courage, nobility, and devotion. He orders that the two 'famous' lovers be buried in the same tomb.

2.2 SCENE SUMMARIES AND CRITICAL COMMENTARY

Act I, Scene i

Summary
At the Egyptian court, Philo and Demetrius, Roman friends of Antony, lament the feminizing effect that Cleopatra has had upon their once great general. When the two lovers enter and Antony, baited by Cleopatra, refuses to hear the messenger sent from Rome by Octavius Caesar, this viewpoint seems confirmed.

Commentary
This scene warrants the closest scrutiny, for it is in many ways – in language, technique, theme – an abstract of the play. In fact, it is like a complete little play in itself as the two Roman soldiers, alone on stage at the beginning and at the end, frame, as it were, the tableau of Antony and Cleopatra's spectacular entrance and exit. Philo's 'Look where they come--/ Take but good note' (10-11) invites us, as well as Demetrius, to view the scene through his eyes. The near anonymity

of these soldiers – they do not appear, at least by name, elsewhere in the play – makes what they have to say seem representative of the common opinion of Rome which sees in Antony one of the triple pillars of the world 'transformed' in Egypt 'Into a strumpet's fool' (12-13). Philo's introductory speech is a paradox of language as it points to an Antony more mythic than human, the great warrior who 'glowed like plated Mars' in his resplendent armour, at the same time as it disparages him in the most vulgar terms as being no more than the 'bellows and the fan / To cool a gypsy's lust'. The word 'gypsy' derives from 'Egyptian', and in Shakespeare's day all gypsies were thought to come ultimately from that country. To Philo the only plausible explanation for Antony's 'devotion' (5) to such an obviously inferior person must be his 'dotage' (1): the word plays on Antony's advancing age, his 'dotage', and with it his foolish 'doting', as if his *doting* on Cleopatra were in itself confirmation of his *dotage*, or his *dotage* responsible for his *doting*. The description of Cleopatra as 'tawny' (6) in complexion associates her with common Renaissance belief that the dark-skinned inhabitants of Africa were inordinately 'lascivious' (see Caesar's use of that word at I.iv.56).

Although the eunuchs' fans wafting over Cleopatra pick up Philo's image of Antony as 'the fan / To cool a gypsy's lust' and ironically associate him with these neutered servants of the queen, the first appearance of the two lovers does not necessarily bear out the soldier's contemptuous description of them. As Philo speaks, a '*Flourish*' is heard – the standard fanfare of trumpets on the Jacobean stage to indicate the entrance of royal figures. Since Antony is an emperor and Cleopatra a queen, they may be wearing, in this ceremonious entrance, royal regalia; Cleopatra, certainly, would not *look* the 'gypsy'. The bustling activity of their entrance does suggest an 'o'erflowing' of 'measure' (1-2); but it is exciting, not disgusting.

What transpires after the entrance of Antony and Cleopatra confirms Philo in a way, but in a different light. True, Antony is given to 'great devotion', but he never appears debauched. And Cleopatra emerges as a complex figure, holding Antony in her power, yes, but aware of the vulnerability that comes from investing so much love in one person and thus fearful that Antony might heed the call of Rome's messenger and leave her as he left Fulvia. This scene cautions us, then, that it would be a mistake to dismiss Cleopatra as a mere lustful 'gypsy'. After Philo's grim 'Behold and see' (13), the next four lines (14-17) spoken by the lovers suggest a liturgical antiphon and response. To be sure, Cleopatra's request of Antony, 'If it be love indeed, tell me how much', is her way of teasing him and thereby proving her dominance over him, as Philo suggests; but it also mocks the Roman worship of 'measure' (2). Antony's answer is, indeed, Egyptian in its excess, in its 'o'erflowing': 'There's beggary in the love that can be reckoned' – but is Antony wrong? Is it possible to 'reckon' ('measure') love? Or to 'set a bourn' to it, as Cleopatra, again mocking Roman values, goes on to propose? Antony's reply – 'Then must thou needs find out new heaven, new earth' – is, like Philo's 'Behold and see', biblical (Revelations, 21:1) but without blasphemy, for Antony echoes lovers of all ages attesting the transforming powers of love.

Antony's refusal to hear the messenger 'from Rome' (18) astonishes Demetrius and shows us why Rome has concluded that 'The triple pillar of the world' has shed all concern for affairs of empire. Cleopatra uses every device, from playing on his pride to inflaming his passion, to keep him from listening; and she succeeds. For Antony not to listen to the messenger is a personal rebuke to Caesar himself. Whereas another man might respond with annoyance to taunts of subservience to a 'shrill-tongued' (32) wife and a 'scarce-bearded' (21) rival, Antony laughs them off; everything about Cleopatra is charming to him:

> Fie, wrangling queen!
> Whom everything becomes – to chide, to laugh,
> To weep; whose every passion fully strives
> To make itself, in thee, fair and admired!   (48-51)

This, to be sure, is not exactly the Cleopatra whom we have seen on stage so far; and Antony seems oblivious to her own 'shrill' voice. As members of the audience, we either accept her at this point, as Antony does, on faith, condemn her as Philo does, or suspend judgement altogether. The last is the wisest course for the moment.

The entertainment that Antony proposes for the evening, to 'wander through the streets and note / The qualities of people' (53-4), while less regal than common, is not in itself an indication of debauchery. Philo and Demetrius are indeed offended by the wrongheadedness that allows Antony to discuss an evening's pleasure instead of attending to the messenger; but it is his declaration of indifference to the empire and his dedication to love that seals their opinion of him. One can imagine the disgust on the Roman faces as Antony utters the first of many images, associated throughout the play with Egypt, of melting, dissolving, the withering away of boundaries:

> Let Rome in Tiber melt, and the wide arch
> Of the ranged empire fall! Here is my space.
> Kingdoms are clay: our dungy earth alike
> Feeds man as beast. The nobleness of life
> Is to do thus...

Whereupon he encircles Cleopatra in his arms and kisses her (33-6). For the audience these lines may confirm the Roman view, or they may show how restrictive and life-denying that view is. At the very least their poetry places Antony among those who 'hear music' and Philo and Demetrius among those who do not. With whom is the reader or spectator to side?

Act I, Scene ii

Summary
Cleopatra's attendants tease one another and banter with a Soothsayer; but the playful mood is broken when the Queen rushes in to look for Antony, who has suddenly turned serious. She will not stay to 'look upon him', however, as he enters with a messenger, who brings him news of a conspiracy by his wife Fulvia and his brother Lucius against Caesar and of an uprising in another part of the empire. A second messenger brings news of Fulvia's death, and Antony swears to Enobarbus that he is determined to 'break' from Cleopatra and return to Rome.

Commentary
The playful beginning of this scene contrasts sharply with the preceding scene, in which Antony voices his feelings for Cleopatra as the most exalted love and Philo regards these feelings as mere lust. That both speak in poetry may indicate that a 'Roman' seriousness informs Antony's love for Cleopatra just as it does Philo's dedication to Rome; but whereas Antony can respond to both claims, Philo can see only perversity or dishonour in the acknowledgement of any claim that rivals Rome. But here Cleopatra's attendants, speaking in the lightest of prose, voice neither extreme: instead, they revel in the joy of sexuality, without moral reproach or idealistic exaltation, spicing their dialogue with double meanings and bawdy innuendoes. Their levity may seem to confirm Rome's view of Egypt, but the sheer fun of this dialogue should warn us against making too hasty a judgement. One could argue, instead, that something wholesome is going on: the good-humoured joking of Charmian, Iras, and Alexas abounds with images of fertility ('the o'erflowing Nilus'), procreation, and birth – all life-affirming. Significantly, the eunuch Mardian and the Roman soldiers do not join in. The Egyptian ribaldry may be a less than adequate expression of Antony's feelings, although the play repeatedly alludes to the sexual attraction between the two lovers, but the Roman reticence may point to an uneasiness about sex itself. Even the Soothsayer's prognostications (16, 31, 33), playful in themselves, contribute to the serious undercurrent of the scene and foreshadow the ending of the play.

In the First Folio, Enobarbus's 'Hush! Here comes Anthony' (79) follows the direction '*Enter* CLEOPATRA'. This could be a mistake or simply mean that Cleopatra is heard approaching before she is seen, but it is also possible that Shakespeare intends Enorbarbus to be ironical: Antony has become Cleopatra by losing his identity to her. The light mood of the scene abruptly changes when Cleopatra rushes in looking for Antony, fearing the 'Roman thought' that 'on the sudden . . . hath struck him' and dispelled his 'mirth' (82-3). 'Roman thought' is ambiguous: either Cleopatra understands that Antony is now thinking about his responsibilities to Rome, in contrast to his behaviour in the first scene, or she regards any serious-minded thought as axiomatically 'Roman'. Her fear of Antony's sudden change of mood casts an interesting light on her own behaviour in the preceding scene where she mocked his magniloquent profession of love by taunting him with having married Fulvia and not loving her (I.i.41). Later in this scene Antony will speak of 'These strong Egyptian fetters' (117) that bind him to her; but clearly Cleopatra is just as bound to Antony: politically, because as queen of a nation conquered by Rome she needs Antony as a buffer against Caesar, but emotionally, too. In contrast to the Romans' one-sided view of her as a 'gypsy' or 'whore', Shakespeare's portrait is much more complex: Cleopatra is a mature, experienced woman of the world, fully aware of the fickleness of which men are capable and of the hazards of fortune; life has made her shrewd, but it has also made her insecure. Her refusal to see Antony after she has just rushed in looking for him may be no more than a ploy on her part to keep her dominance by playing hard to get; but, if he has seen her as he enters, he is too absorbed in his 'Roman thought' to notice. Ironically, as the scene ends, he will ask for 'leave to part' (181) – what, undoubtedly, she had been fearing most.

Antony now sees the messenger from Rome; and throughout this scene he compels admiration for desiring to know the truth about himself (106-10:'Speak to me home...'). His startling use of Philo's word 'dotage' (118; see I.i.1) is his clearest recognition of what is happening to him; there is a touch of the heroic – the old Antony – as he utters it, as there is a few lines later when he confesses how remiss he had been in failing to recognize Fulvia's 'great spirit' (123). He reacts to the news of her death by wishing to 'break off' from 'this enchanting queen' (129).

Left alone, Antony calls for Enobarbus, who, as Antony's close friend, is near the centre of the tragedy but yet sees himself as an impartial judge – ironic, sceptical, objective. Enobarbus's gibes are not unlike Cleopatra's earlier, but his reflect the conflict within Antony: Cleopatra does, after all, hold Antony in 'fetters', and his problem is to balance the claims of Egypt with those of Rome. Antony's answers are not lightly given – he speaks in verse, Enobarbus in prose – as he reasserts his soldiership: 'Let our officers / Have notice what we purpose' (178-9). Antony's essential decency is further proved by his nowhere blaming Cleopatra for the 'ills' that his own 'idleness doth hatch' (130-1); he blames his own 'dotage'. The business that Fulvia 'hath broachèd in the state' (173) necessitates his returning to Rome to heal the rift with Caesar, but his seriousness throughout the scene indicates that he has never really made a 'break' from Rome. Given the depth of his love for Cleopatra, however, he may now be making a break that he will not be able to endure. The heroic choice between love and honour, Egypt and Rome, may not be for him a choice at all.

Act I, Scene iii

Summary
Cleopatra grows increasingly desperate to keep Antony near her. Antony informs her that Fulvia is dead and that he must return to Rome to heal the 'garboils' or civil war that 'she awaked' there. Cleopatra at first accuses him of false love; but, seeing that he is determined to answer the call of 'honour', she wishes him 'laurel victory, and smooth success'.

Commentary
Cleopatra is very coquettish in this scene; we do not see her at her best as she desperately connives at ways to hold on to Antony. Her attendant Charmian advises her not to 'Tempt' Antony 'too far' by her contrariness (11), but for much of the scene Cleopatra seems almost to enjoy playing the melodramatic role of a 'queen / So mightily betrayed!' (24-5). Even as she is aware of her own role-playing, she ironically accuses Antony of 'excellent dissembling' (79). Antony courteously hears her out, yet he is not, as before, amused by her coquettishness: 'The strong necessity of time commands' his return to Rome, he tells her (42). Cleopatra does not give up easily, but in a remarkable turn-around she reveals new depths to her character: realizing that she has played her last card and lost, with shrewdness and yet with a true ring of sincerity, she abruptly changes her tone when she sees that her taunting no longer charms Antony. Unlike Dido, who cursed Aeneas for leaving her for Rome, Cleopatra, suddenly subdued (a new role?), wishes that 'all the gods go with' Antony (99). When she tells him that 'Your honour calls you hence' (97), she senses at last that in Antony's character the Roman code of 'honour' is innate and essential.

Although Antony is firm with her, his last words make clear that both Rome and Egypt have equal claims on him; wherever he goes, she remains with him; but, until the end of the scene, she is slow to realize that he departs as *her* 'soldier, servant, making peace or war' as *she* chooses (70-1). It is *only* as her 'soldier, servant' (lover) that he can balance both claims, as if she makes worthwhile all the responsibilities that Rome lays upon him.

Act 1, Scene iv

Summary
In Rome, Antony's fellow triumvirs, Caesar and Lepidus, discuss Antony's absence at a time when the Triumvirate needs him. While Lepidus tries to smooth things over, Caesar contrasts the 'womanly' character that Antony has become with the great soldier he once was. A messenger announces that Pompey and two 'famous pirates', Menecrates and Menas, have taken control of the seas and that Pompey's name alone is attracting many followers in Rome. Caesar laments that Antony has forgotton his 'honour' in such a dire moment, but he and Lepidus pledge support to one another.

Commentary
The political action of the play begins with our first view of Octavius Caesar, who symbolizes Rome's claim upon Antony as Cleopatra does Egypt's. In the previous scene, Cleopatra attempted to lure Antony from 'the strong necessity of time', but Caesar seems to stand almost for time itself as he complains how Antony confounds 'such time / That drums him from his sport' (28-9). When he observes that it is not his 'natural vice to hate / Our great competitor' (2-3), 'competitor' here only means 'partner' (in the Triumvirate); but the word carries the suggestion of 'competition' and indicates how Caesar really views Antony in relation to himself. (Antony, on the other hand, will use the word 'partner' at II.ii.59.) To Lepidus's contention that Antony's 'faults' are not 'Evils enow to darken all his goodness' (11-12), Caesar replies, 'You are too indulgent' (16). The play makes much of Caesar's youth as opposed to Antony's age, but Caesar seems to have been born old, as when he compares his older rival to 'boys' who should know better but let 'their present pleasure' overrule their 'judgement' (31-3). Can one imagine this puritanical young man, so sure of his own judgements, fishing, drinking, and wasting 'The lamps of night in revel' (4-5)? Everything that Antony does even innocently seems distorted and vulgar as Caesar describes his activities. But, despite Caesar's assured moral stance, the whole scene tends to undercut almost everything that he is saying; for, even as he calls upon Antony to 'Leave thy lascivious wassails' (56), Antony is already on his way back to Rome to reclaim both 'time' and 'honour'.

The news of Pompey's gathering strength and popularity elicits from Caesar, who now needs Antony's forces to help meet the threat to the Triumvirate, a remarkable speech (56-71) in which he recalls an almost mythic Antony, the great Roman soldier, who once at Modena turned defeat into a kind of personal victory as he overcame famine by eating and drinking such repugnant things as 'some did die to look on'. Caesar's admiration is unmistakable here, as he recognizes in his 'competitor' the soldier he himself never could be. But irony is at work too; for what Caesar fails to understand is that this Antony, who so heroically and with 'honour' defied bitter fortune, is of a piece with the Antony who 'O'erflows the measure' in Egypt. As a soldier and as a lover, Antony responds to life with his total being, whether at the extremes of pain or pleasure, honour or love.

The scene ends with Caesar's pledging to allow Lepidus to 'be partaker' (83) in the 'business' (80) against Pompey. Without Antony, Caesar needs all the help he can get. The irony of the last line, 'I know it for my bond', will be made clear later when he betrays both Lepidus and Antony.

Act I, Scene v

Summary
In Alexandria, Cleopatra finds time heavy without Antony, who is still on his way to Rome. She thinks constantly about him. Daily she sends him messages; and Alexas, one of her servants, returns from Antony with a pearl that he has double-kissed and with a promise to 'piece / Her opulent throne with kingdoms'.

Commentary
A languorous, playful scene follows the serious one at Rome. It underscores not only Cleopatra's anxiety during Antony's absence but also the depth of her feeling for him; she wishes to drink mandragora so that she 'might sleep out this great gap of time / My Antony is away' (5-6) – the line foreshadows the end of the play. The sexual banter between Cleopatra and her attendants stands in contrast to the contempt for sensuality in Caesar's strictures on Antony. But, for all her playfulness, Cleopatra betrays her deeper feelings, as when she teases her eunuch Mardian; he, at least, does not have to let his thoughts stray outside Egypt as hers do. Mardian's reply, 'Yet have I fierce affections, and think / What Venus did with Mars' (17-18), plays on both aspects of the word 'affections': deep feelings as well as sexual yearnings. In the context of the play, his answer is double-edged: Venus and Mars made passionate love together, but from a 'Roman' viewpoint Mars, the god of war, lay down his arms for Venus, the goddess of love, and thus, in a sense, was emasculated, as the Romans think Antony was by Cleopatra.

Cleopatra makes no response to Mardian but, instead, begins to daydream about Antony in lines that foreshadow her great dream of him in the final scene of the play. Her evocation of Antony (19-26) as

'The demi-Atlas of this earth' completes and transcends Caesar's
tribute in the preceding scene. There Caesar recalled the rugged
soldier who outwitted fortune, but here Cleopatra evokes the
classical image of the 'compleat' warrior, soldier *and* lover, fully
armed and mounted on his 'happy horse'. The image of the horse
'happy . . . to bear the weight of Antony!' carries a sexual connota-
tion, and the entire passage combines in harmony the values of Rome
and Egypt (see 'Themes'). As Cleopatra imagines Antony affection-
ately calling for his 'serpent of old Nile' (25), the earlier image of
drinking mandragora to numb her while Antony is away turns into
'most delicious poison' (27) with which she now feeds herself:
thinking of him, even though his absence is painful (or poison) to her,
restores her to life.

And then a very strange thing happens: without a pause, and in no
way underplaying her 'affections' for Antony, Cleopatra's thoughts
open out to the other renowned lovers in her life – Julius Caesar and
'great Pompey'. With humorous self-assurance, she pictures herself
as a goddess of love whom even the sun has darkened (see Commentary on 'tawny', I.i.6) and 'wrinkled' with his 'amorous pinches'
(28-9). Luckily, no Roman is present; he would be shocked by her
joyous delight in her own sexual appeal. We should contrast Caesar's
somewhat priggish dismissal of sex with Cleopatra's boast here of
herself as 'A morsel for a monarch' (31): sex to her is as natural as
eating.

Suddenly, Cleopatra's almost trance-like state is broken by the
entrance of Alexas, one of the many messengers whom she daily
sends to Antony. Her thoughts immediately return to Antony,
elevating him above even Julius Caesar and Pompey. Experience has
taught Alexas how to deal with his 'dear queen', whom he grandly
addresses as 'Sovereign of Egypt, hail!' (34) – reminding us that he is
addressing no ordinary person. A skilful diplomat, aware of how
whimsical his mistress can be, he weighs his words with extreme care
in the dialogue that follows since he cannot be sure what answer she
wants when she asks him whether Antony is 'sad, or merry' (50). We
may recall how dismayed she was earlier when a 'Roman thought'
drove away Antony's 'mirth' (I.ii.82-3). Alexas's reply is vague
enough for Cleopatra to complete the picture that she really wants of
Antony:

> O heavenly mingle! Be'st thou sad or merry,
> The violence of either thee becomes,
> So does it no man else.   (59-61)

We may laugh at her justifications for wanting Antony neither sad
nor merry, for admiring his 'well-divided disposition' (53, 55-8); but
her imaginings and Alexas's report together capture Antony in

perfect fulfilment of his role, here and now, in this life, as heroic soldier and lover. Cleopatra had imagined Antony as 'demi-Atlas' mounted on his horse, thinking of her as he prepared for battle. Alexas now reports that Antony, after kissing many times the 'orient pearl' that he was sending back to her, 'soberly did mount an arm-gaunt steed' (39-50). 'Soberly' is a 'Roman' word, like 'Roman thought', but it describes an image of Antony on his horse that realizes Cleopatra's own earlier image in her mind. She had called that horse 'happy' 'to bear the weight of Antony'; in neighing 'so high', the horse would seem to confirm that image of happiness and pride. Imagination and reality become one here. Physically, Antony is somewhere between Rome and Egypt; metaphorically also, he is between the two, maintaining at last the values of each in perfect balance. Antony at this moment is what he calls himself, 'firm Roman', resolute and faithful, and given a sense of purpose by 'great Egypt', who gives heart to his Roman greatness.

At the same time, Antony has made Cleopatra's life more meaningful, too: his 'tinct' gilds her as it does Alexas (37). Charmian is less diplomatic than Alexas in her response to Cleopatra's question whether she did 'Ever love Caesar' as much as she now does Antony (66-7). When Charmian reminds her that she did not always 'sing' this way, Cleopatra attributes her earlier praises of Caesar to the irresponsible utterings of her 'salad days, / When I was green in judgement, cold in blood' (73-4). To Caesar she was indeed a 'morsel for a monarch', but just a morsel; her obsession with Antony betrays the deeper 'affections', and with them the deeper anxieties, that make lovers vulnerable to one another. (Her two former lovers sexually 'died' for her – see the pun at 33 – but then they both returned to Rome forever.) Her determination to 'unpeople Egypt' before she runs out of messengers to Antony recalls his earlier 'Let Rome in Tiber melt' (I.i.33); at that time she mocked his 'Excellent falsehood!'; but now she, too, claims that she would give up the world before she would give up Antony.

Act II, Scene i

Summary

Pompey plots to overturn the ruling parties in Rome and to make himself sole emperor. He is confident that 'the libertine' Antony will not leave Egypt, that Caesar commands no loyalty among the masses, and that Lepidus is ineffectual. His officer Varrius enters to announce that Antony is expected 'every hour in Rome'. Menas hopes that Caesar and Antony will not be able to reconcile their differences although Pompey thinks that fear of him may unite them.

Commentary
This scene introduces Pompey, whose uprising necessitates Antony's
return to Rome. Pompey is one of the interesting subordinate
characters in the play; he appears in few scenes, but in these he is
vividly sketched. The scene makes clear what a mediocre man he is,
but he has prestige simply because he is the son of Pompey the Great.
Curious complications underlie his present motives: he admits that he
is a suitor 'to their throne' but at the same time regards this glittering
prize as losing its worth the more time passes (4–5). He shares the
view of Antony as a debauched 'amorous surfeiter' (33), who, 'In
Egypt sits at dinner' (11–12) – an image that recalls Cleopatra's boast
of being 'a morsel for a monarch'; but the implication here is cynical
and vulgar. He recognizes Antony's greatness as a soldier: 'his
soldiership / Is twice the other twain' (34–5) – an observation that
casts light on the earlier scene with Caesar and Lepidus (I.iv) and
their need for Antony's return. When he says, 'The people love me,
and the sea is mine' (9), he seems to sense that his 'powers are
crescent' at this moment only because Antony has not yet joined his
fellow triumvirs, Caesar is not popular, and Lepidus is of no account
(10–16).

The unexpected news that 'Mark Antony is every hour in Rome /
Expected' (29–30) brings home one of the major themes of the play:
the arrogance and fallibility of human judgement. Pompey is
surprised that so great a soldier as Antony should even bother to
enter 'such a petty war' (34). He does not understand that Antony's
decision to leave Egypt transcends the importance of the war itself; it
is a decision to reclaim 'honour'.

Act II, Scene ii

Summary
The three rulers of Rome – Caesar, Lepidus, and Antony – meet
together for the first time in the play and, after airing their differences, are reconciled and agree to join forces against Pompey.
Agrippa, one of Caesar's party, proposes that the renewed friendship
be cemented by the marriage of Antony, now a widower, to Caesar's
widowed sister Octavia – a proposal on which the two triumvirs join
hands. Left alone with Agrippa and Maecenas, another of Caesar's
subordinates, Enobarbus tells of the hedonistic life that the Roman
soldiers lead in Egypt and describes the first meeting of Antony and
Cleopatra.

Commentary
From the start, this intensely political scene belongs to Antony,
belying earlier descriptions of him as 'womanly' or as a truant to
honour. He allows Caesar to reproach him but at the same time

forces his younger partner into a corner: 'Scarce-bearded Caesar' (I.i.21) seems unable or unwilling to pluck 'Antonio's beard' (7). Antony has returned to Rome in the mood for political reconciliation, but without debasement to himself. Throughout the scene we catch glimpses of the great 'captain' acclaimed by the Romans before he went to Egypt: Agrippa, Caesar's own officer and friend, refers to Antony as 'the best of men' (130). Despite all Roman criticism of him earlier, Antony seems in his element in Rome. Although there is some amusing formality between the two triumvirs as they enter from separate stage doors and speak to their own officers before acknowledging one another (13-27), Antony seizes the initiative by confronting Caesar directly (29-30; 35-6). Caesar lamely accuses him of practising 'on my state' through the conspiracy of 'Your wife and brother' (38-44); but, as we already know from I.ii, Antony is free from blame in this regard, and he reminds Caesar that he has satisfied him by letter on this matter. In effect, he is telling Caesar that if he is looking for an excuse to quarrel he will have to come up with something better (45-54). Caesar next mentions the messenger whom Antony had slighted. Antony admits this neglect; but he had, after all, seen him the 'next day . . . which was as much / As to have asked him pardon'; the messenger is hardly worth a war: 'Let this fellow / Be nothing of our strife', says Antony (74-81). When Caesar next accuses him of breaking his oath to supply him with 'arms and aid', Antony, again with dignity, takes personal blame; but, in doing so, he does not debase himself (81-98). Lepidus, almost forgotten but hovering over the scene, seizes an opportunity to re-enter the conversation; and he urges peace.

Although a reconciliation takes place, Enobarbus sees things more realistically (indicated by the switch to prose in his speech, 102-7). As long as Caesar and Antony need one another against Pompey, he urges them to 'borrow one another's love for the instant'. Later, when they have defeated their common enemy, he says, they can fall to wrangling again. But Antony, who has made a deliberate effort to leave Egypt for Rome and thus restore his 'honour', silences his friend (108; compare I.ii.178: 'No more light answers'). For all his 'realism', Enobarbus fails to see that for Antony the choice is not between Rome and Egypt. Antony's dilemma is to keep the two in harmony. Caesar, however, clearly sees that too great a temperamental difference exists between him and Antony for any bond between them to hold long.

To allay Caesar's doubts about the reconciliation, Agrippa proposes marriage between Antony and Octavia as a means of knitting their 'hearts / With an unslipping knot' (126–30). The proposal is no more than a political manoeuvre – 'studied' even before this meeting, 'not a present thought' (139). Agrippa's idea that 'Her love to both / Would each to other, and all loves to both, / Draw after her'

(136-8) is a happy wish, but one wonders whether such an arrangement can effect a lasting improvement in relations between men so fundamentally different. Antony refuses to commit himself until he knows what 'power' Caesar has to bring about this marriage; and, once he is reassured, he wants this 'business', as he calls it, dispatched 'ere we put ourselves in arms' (140-67). It is easy to judge Antony's behaviour as cynical, but the play constantly warns us against making hasty judgements. Although a Renaissance audience would regard a loveless marriage as the usual means of bringing about alliances among the great, the scene makes a telling point in Shakespeare's examination of Roman honour and Egyptian love: Antony in Rome does as the Romans do; and, if sensuality is the excess of the Egyptian virtue, heartlessness is the excess of the Roman virtue. Taking the whole view of him, we can see Antony here acting *in*, not *out* of, character.

A trenchant comment now comes from Enobarbus, alone on the stage with Caesar's two subordinates, in his famous description of Cleopatra (191-241). By reminding us of her at the end of this scene of political jockeying, he confirms how fragile the reconciliation actually is. Enobarbus is the only one in the play, besides Antony, with a foot in both worlds, Rome and Egypt; and, like all the Romans, he is fascinated by the East. Whether Enobarbus is bragging, telling the truth, or just laying it on thick as he describes the 'o'erflowing', measureless world of Egypt where the day is for sleeping and the night made 'light with drinking' (178-9) is hard to tell. There is an element of music hall here with Agrippa and Maecenas as straight men to Enobarbus's comedy routine. Yet, once he starts his report of Cleopatra's first meeting with Antony, it becomes apparent that he is enthralled by her (confirmed by his switching from prose to verse). Agrippa's paradoxical exclamation, 'Royal wench!' (227), in reaction to what he is hearing, is apt; for the whole speech is one great paradox, combining art and nature in delicate balance to describe a phenomenon who beggars 'all description', whom fans heat and cool at the same time, who breathless still breathes, whose 'infinite variety' custom cannot 'stale', and who, above all, makes 'defect perfection'. When Enobarbus observes that 'Other women cloy / The appetites they feed, but she makes hungry / Where most she satisfies', the imagery of feeding that the Romans tend to associate with mere sexual satisfaction takes on transcendent value. Everyone feels the power of this 'Rare Egyptian' (219), this goddess of love, of life itself. Enobarbus's own rapture in some way vindicates Antony.

The scene takes place in Rome, yet ends – in another paradox – with a magnificent evocation of Cleopatra. The proposed marriage of Antony to Octavia is the political climax of the scene, but the Queen of Egypt dominates the ending. Maecenas describes

Octavia in what should be appealing abstractions – 'beauty, wisdom, modesty' (242); but these pale in comparison to the rich particulars that Enobarbus cites to describe Cleopatra.

Act II, Scene iii

Summary
Antony assures Octavia that, despite the negative reports she has heard, he will be a good husband. The Soothsayer, whom we had met earlier at Cleopatra's court (I.ii), warns Antony that his 'lustre thickens' or dulls when he is near Caesar and urges him to 'hie...to Egypt again'. Antony acknowledges that Caesar will always win over him in Fortune's game and vows to return to Egypt in spite of his forthcoming marriage to Octavia and what he said to her at the beginning of the scene.

Commentary
This short scene immediately confirms Enobarbus's insight at the close of the previous scene, that Antony will 'never' leave Cleopatra. In the space of only forty-three lines, we witness a complete turnaround in Antony – not for the first time in the play (see I.i and I.ii), but never before so rapidly. Like the previous scene, this one also takes place in Rome and ends with thoughts of 'the East', where Antony's 'pleasure lies' (41). Throughout this scene, Antony is tense and insecure, whereas, in the last scene, he had seemed in command in dealing with Caesar. It is difficult to account for the sudden change, but the dialogue with the Soothsayer makes clear that Caesar is as compelling to Antony as Cleopatra is. Antony's 'daemon' or guardian spirit may be, as the Soothsayer claims, 'Noble, courageous, high, unmatchable, / Where Caesar's is not' (20-2); but 'that natural luck' (27) of Caesar's dims Antony's lustrous qualities when they are together. Antony refuses to discuss these things with the Soothsayer and sends him out to find Ventidius, with whom he will be more at ease discussing military matters. Left alone, however, Antony tells himself, in one of his few soliloquies, that even at the most trivial 'sports' Caesar is always the winner: 'The very dice obey him' (33-9). Does he believe this? Or he is looking for an excuse to go back to Egypt? Or does Caesar unconsciously frighten him ('near him thy angel / Becomes afeared, as being o'erpowered', 22-3)?

Before he leaves the stage, the Soothsayer says to Antony, 'I say again, thy spirit / Is all afraid to govern thee near him [Caesar]; /But he away, 'tis noble' (29-31). Yet, Antony's noble bearing in the previous scene seems to call these words into question. There, as we saw, Antony more than held his own with Caesar. One way of understanding the new, self-doubting Antony is to consider what occurs before his encounter with the Soothsayer. The scene begins with Antony's first interview with his prospective bride. The stage direction illustrates without ambiguity what the marriage means in political terms: '*Enter* ANTONY *and* CAESAR, *with* OCTAVIA *between them*'. Ironically, Antony's first words to his betrothed are about the inevitable separations that his duties as a triumvir will bring about between them; he will not be home very much! (Compare his departure from Cleopatra, I.iii.102-4, where he indicates that their separation is only physical, not spiritual.) Antony's imagery is pure 'Roman': acknowledging that he has 'not kept my square', he vows to act in the future 'by the rule' (6-7). Nothing that he says 'O'erflows the measure' (I.i.2). A more loveless scene between a groom and his bride would be hard to come by. Once the 'business' that Antony wanted completed in the last scene is over, they go their separate ways. Caesar's only words in the entire dialogue of nine lines are 'Good night' (9).

The words of the Soothsayer urging Antony to return to Egypt obviously strike a chord. Antony has deluded himself into thinking that this marriage will satisfy Rome's claim on him; but now he realizes that, although he is making 'this marriage for my peace, / I' the East my pleasure lies' (40-1). What the Soothsayer says may seem distressing on the surface, but Antony may be hearing what he wants to hear so that he can justify to himself his return to Egypt, where his 'lustre' (28) will shine once again. Perhaps, too, Antony is using the Soothsayer's comments about Caesar's 'natural luck' to excuse himself for having violated the Egyptian part of his nature by betraying Cleopatra. To leave Octavia now, however, would dishonour him and enrage Caesar; thus the marriage, even before it takes place, is a kind of trap. (Did Caesar intend that?) Antony seems to be talking himself into defeat, and only the entrance of Ventidius rouses him: to discuss the military situation in Parthia comes as a relief from contradictory feelings. Antony's dilemma, trying to reconcile the conflicting claims of love and honour, makes his situation tragic. To return to Egypt, he would have to surrender the greatness that gives him identity in the world at large; but to stay in Rome, he would have to deny powerful feelings that alone make his private life meaningful. By contrast, Caesar has no conflict; he seems not even to have a private life.

Act II, Scene iv

Summary
Lepidus, Maecenas, and Agrippa discuss the long journey to Mount Misenum, where they will meet with Pompey.

Commentary
The last scene ended with Antony vowing to return to Egypt where

his 'pleasure lies'; but this scene reminds us that larger political stakes demand his involvement and loyalty. Agrippa, loyal to Caesar, notes that if 'Mark Antony / Will e'en but kiss Octavia,...we'll follow' (2-3). Leaving the public sphere where he plays such an important role will not be easy for Antony. The scene is extremely short, but it conveys a sense of the epic distances covered in the play.

Act II, Scene v

Summary
Without Antony, Cleopatra is bored. She reminisces about the happy times that she and Antony have shared. A messenger 'from Italy' brings news of Antony's reconciliation with Caesar and marriage to Octavia. In her fury, Cleopatra strikes and threatens the messenger. But she does not yet admit defeat and gives orders to find out what Octavia looks like.

Commentary
The languorous, playful beginning of this scene at Alexandria comes as an interlude amidst the Roman scenes of political intrigue. However badly Antony may have appeared in going ahead with his purely political marriage while at the same time acknowledging that he will return to Cleopatra, we at least see in this scene the depth of feeling that Cleopatra has for him; he will be returning to someone who cares passionately about him, just as he does for her. Furthermore, in contrasting Cleopatra with the statuesque Octavia, the scene illustrates the 'infinite variety' that Enobarbus had attributed to her (II.ii.237); she is by turns wistful, playful, bawdy, enraged, despondent, hopeful, ashamed, subdued and mournful. If she is here not quite the goddess whom Enobarbus had described, her liveliness reveals her as the 'wrangling queen' whom Antony had said 'every thing becomes' (I.i.48-52).

Cleopatra's bawdy dialogue with her attendant Charmian and the eunuch Mardian (at his expense since she does not want to play billiards with him – a game involving poking balls into a pocket) contrasts sharply with the 'still' conversation of the 'modest' Octavia. The banter lifts her melancholy spirits and leads her to reminiscing about happier times when she would laugh Antony 'out of patience' and back 'into patience' (19-20). Once, she 'drunk him to his bed' and dressed him in her head dresses ('tires') and 'mantles' while she 'wore his sword Philippan' (15-23)–the sword he had used in defeating Brutus and Cassius at Philippi. Seen from the Roman point of view, Cleopatra here is an enchantress who, in Caesar's word (I.iv.7), had made Antony 'womanly' by forcing him to lose his identity. But there is no sting in what she says; she sorely misses him.

The news from Rome makes for even more comedy as Cleopatra, determined to hear what she wants to hear about Antony, anticipates the messenger's words and reads meanings into his facial expressions, barely giving him a chance to deliver his report. But the comedy builds up suspense, for we know what news the messenger brings. When it is at last out, her fury knows no bounds: '*She hales him up and down*' is an original stage direction from the First Folio. Although Charmian reminds her, and she herself acknowledges later, that the messenger is himself innocent, she acts as if she is taking revenge upon Antony. But such is her complexity that even in acting so furiously (albeit comically too) she realizes that she is also acting ignobly 'since I myself / Have given myself the cause' (83-4) – that is, she is to blame for loving Antony as much as she does. Charmian reminds her how earlier (I.v.66-72) she had dispraised Julius Caesar in praising Antony, and Cleopatra readily confesses that 'I am paid for 't now' (108-10). At the same time, having vented her fury, she cares too much about Antony to simply give him up: 'Let him for ever go! – Let him not' (116) movingly expresses her confusion, her dilemma. Antony had once said of her that 'She is cunning past man's thought' (I.ii.147), and now Cleopatra proves how resourceful she can be: she is going to find out everything she can about Octavia – her years, her 'inclination' or character, even the 'colour of her hair'; if Octavia cannot match her charms, then there is still hope.

The ending of the scene is surprisingly subdued given the violence of so much of it. Cleopatra asks to be alone in her grief, which certainly seems genuine, although even in the next to last line she is wondering about Octavia's height – the tone is wonderfully complex. Not once has she said anything about the political consequences for her of Antony's marriage to Caesar's sister; the loss of Antony, not the possible loss of her kingdom, is the cause of her rage and grief.

Act II, Scene vi

Summary
Near Misenum, Caesar, Lepidus, and Antony meet with Pompey, who consents, somewhat hastily, to a treaty that does not favour him. Pompey then suggests that the four leaders draw lots to begin a round of feasting in celebration of their concord. Left alone on stage, Enobarbus and Menas agree that Pompey is probably finished now as a political force and that Antony's marriage to Octavia was made strictly for 'policy' rather than for 'love'.

Commentary
With this scene and the next, the Pompey affair is resolved; it remains to be seen whether the conflict between Caesar and Antony will be renewed now that the matter which brought them together has come

to a successful conclusion. From the beginning, Pompey is a defeated man; and clearly, the speed with which he capitulates to the demands of the Triumvirate is a tribute to Antony's presence (a fact that Caesar also counted on); as he admits, 'he did not think. . . . to have met [Antony] here' (49).

Antony's return to Rome was prompted by the call of 'honour' (see I.iii.97); but the *actual* Roman world to which Antony has returned is far from being either 'honourable' or 'great'. Pompey's resentments, as they surface in this scene, give us insights into that world. After his speech (8-23) in which he explains why he took to war (mainly to avenge his 'noble father'), Caesar says, 'Take your time' (23) – a comment as brutal as it is irrelevant. He is reminding Pompey that what he is talking about has nothing to do with the purpose of this meeting – namely, to discuss hostages and to come to terms if war is to be prevented. Caesar begins to emerge as the exemplar of a Roman world that values political expediency, even ruthlessness – values antithetical to Antony's own vision of Rome, the Rome of Julius Caesar and Pompey the Great, not of their lesser descendants. But even Antony, as he fits into this everyday Roman world, does not remain untouched: he marries here for political reasons, and Pompey reminds him that he has cheated him of payment for his father's house in Rome, the house in which Antony now lives.

As in other scenes with the Triumvirate, this one ends with the private conversation of underlings – here Enobarbus and Menas, whose blunt admission (in prose) that they are just 'two thieves' (97) from the opposing sides undermines the high-minded pretensions to diplomacy (in verse) of their betters. The implication seems to be that in war or politics theft is the name of the game. Both agree that Pompey had the worst of the bargain; but, as Menas admits, 'We looked not for Mark Antony here' (108-9). Menas, it turns out, is under the impression that Antony is married to Cleopatra; but, when he hears otherwise, he agrees with Enobarbus that Antony married Octavia for convenience ('occasion') only (133-5). Enobarbus then offers the intriguing insight that Octavia, who is supposed to be the means of bringing Caesar and Antony together, will, because of her 'holy, cold, and still' disposition (125), turn out to be the instrument that sets them quarelling again (129-32). (Could Caesar have foreseen this possibility when he permitted Antony to marry his sister? The question will come up later.) Enobarbus's cynical prophecy that Antony 'will to his Egyptian dish again' (128) voices the customary Roman judgement of Antony's – and Cleopatra's – 'affection' (133) or passion as sexual appetite only. Should we allow ourselves to make this judgement, too?

Act II, Scene vii

Summary
Aboard Pompey's galley, the banquet to celebrate the signing of the
treaty turns into drunken revelry, with Lepidus especially far gone in
his cups. Menas draws Pompey aside to offer him the perfect
opportunity of becoming 'lord of the whole world' – simply by having
the galley set adrift and then cutting the throats of the triumvirs.
Pompey replies that Menas should have carried out that plan without
having told him; now in 'honour', he cannot condone it. Caesar
finally has had enough of the merrymaking; but the others, except for
Menas and Enobarbus, go ashore to continue the revels.

Commentary
An astonishing reversal of images, both aural and visual, occurs in
this scene. Beginning with Philo's condemnation at the play's opening, various Romans have tried to show us Egypt as a place of excess,
luxuriousness, and revelry in contrast to Rome's 'measure', discipline, moderation, and everyday life governed 'by the rule' or
'square'. Yet no Egyptian scene in the play is so marked by excess as
this Roman scene of drunken revelry. The climax of the scene is the
incredible sight (112-22) of the lords of the world – except Lepidus,
who had to be carried off – and their followers joined together by the
ever-cynical Enobarbus in a ring-dance and loudly stamping their feet
to a refrain of a song in tribute to Bacchus, the Roman god of wine
and revelry ('Plumpy Bacchus with pink eyne!'). Pompey observes,
'This is not yet an Alexandrian feast', and Antony comments, 'It
ripens towards it' (100-1); but this Bacchanalian revel fares ill in
comparison with the Egyptian feasts described by Enobarbus in II.ii.
The preceding scene shows Rome's leaders as thieves; this one, as
drunkards, but the overtones are just as dark: Caesar and Antony are
already sparring with one another; both mock Lepidus, who has been
trying to reconcile them (7-9); and Pompey's resentment about
Antony's theft of his father's house surfaces again (131-2). Menas the
'pirate' is the only one who has kept himself 'from the cup' (72), and
in his sobriety he comes up with a plan to kill the triumvirs and make
Pompey sole emperor (68). Only a peculiar sense of 'honour' – one
of Rome's favourite words – keeps Pompey from approving an idea
that he confesses he likes. Pompey's apparent unawareness of the
hypocrisy that Roman honour entails is one of the subtle ways that
Shakespeare uses to show us that Antony cannot be the eventual
winner, for Antony is aware now and again – perhaps, at some level,
always – that 'honour' is not all of a piece. If one version of it makes
him desert Cleopatra for Octavia, another version later causes him to
desert the battle and follow the fleeing Cleopatra at Actium.

The last scene ended with underlings cynically commenting on the main action; this one begins with servants also cynically commenting as they set out '*a banquet*' for their superiors – the drunken rulers of the world (1-18). Lepidus, they note, cannot compete with his fellow triumvirs even in the sphere of drinking, let alone the 'huge sphere'. The '*sennet*' or fanfare of trumpets that announces the entrance of the Triumvirate, Pompey, and '*other captains*' sounds somewhat derisive after the servants' commentary. Antony is the first to speak, and it is ironic that he is in the midst of explaining how the Egyptians measure (an activity associated only with Rome before) 'the flow o' the Nile / By certain scales i' the pyramid' (19-20). The Egyptians, he explains, welcome the overflow of the Nile because its revitalized banks ('the slime and ooze') will 'shortly' provide the 'harvest' (20-5) – a powerful image of life and fertility that bears comparison with Antony's similar image at I.iii.68-71. A few lines later, Antony has a chance to mock the Roman high regard for measurement when he describes by non-description the crocodile to Lepidus as something that 'is shaped, sir, like itself, and it is as broad as it has breadth' (46-54). Antony, though drinking as much as anyone, is in control of himself but still having a good time: Rome and Egypt mingle affably in him. Lepidus is out of control. Caesar is trying to keep up, but he is not having a good time – he does not appreciate the crocodile joke; his 'graver business / Frowns at this levity' (124-5). Antony tells him not to worry, just enjoy the party: 'Be a child o' the time'. Caesar, however, would rather 'possess' time, control it (104-5). (Does Caesar fear the 'Egypt' in him?) As he finds himself losing control, he simply stops and goes his own way, leaving the others to continue the merrymaking on shore.

Act III, Scene i

Summary
Ventidius, sent by Antony at the end of II.iii to subdue the Parthians, is returning from his successful mission, bringing back with him '*the dead body of* PACORUS', the son of the Parthian king. Silius, a Roman soldier, urges Ventidius on to even more ambitious feats so that Antony will accord him a triumphant welcome to Rome. Ventidius, however, wisely reminds Silius that a subordinate officer shows greater discretion by not outshining, and thus not shaming, his superior.

Commentary
After the Roman bacchanal of the preceding scene, Ventidius reminds us that 'these great fellows' (II.vii.137) who rule the world are not gods but ambitious men who fear rivalry. Although men like Ventidius do the actual fighting, their leaders take the glory; in that

sense, war serves the ambitions of men like Caesar and Antony and Pompey. Antony had returned to Rome to answer the call of 'honour' (see I.iii.97), but Rome's political and and military world taints him, too. Magnificent in so many ways, Antony nevertheless is not likely to look too favourably on Ventidius's triumphs if they put him in the shadows.

Ventidius also serves as a kind of choral figure (like Enobarbus, like Eros later) whose own actions comment on Antony's. His 'distinction' (29) is that he combines valour with discretion, a combination that Antony's followers in subsequent scenes will miss in their great captain.

Act III, Scene ii

Summary
Agrippa and Enobarbus mockingly compare Lepidus to a love-sick girl, unable to decide whom she loves most, for the way that he plays up to both Caesar and Antony, plying 'them both with excellent praises'. The Triumvirate enters, with Octavia, as Antony prepares to take her to Athens. Caesar warns Antony to take good care of his sister. Antony replies, with dignity, that he is not to be mistrusted. Torn between brother and husband, Octavia, with tears in her eyes, hardly seems able to speak. Enobarbus, standing aside, observes to Agrippa that Caesar looks as if he is about to weep but is holding himself back. Agrippa replies that Antony is never ashamed to weep. The triumvirs bid farewell to one another, and Antony departs from Rome with Octavia.

Commentary
A scene that emphasizes the valour and discretion of the Roman soldier at his best is followed by one that betrays a disturbing lack of trust and sincerity among the triumvirs. Once again the cynical dialogue of the underlings colours our perspective of the more serious dialogue of their 'betters'.

The three emperors of the Roman world now enter together – for the last time in the play – with Octavia; and it is apparent that she occupies the same position between Caesar and Antony as does Lepidus . Like his, her role is to keep the fragile bond of friendship between them from breaking apart. Antony compares her to a 'swan's-down feather' that floats upright – 'neither way inclines' – 'upon the swell' of the tide (48-50). The image is ominous; the tide could quickly turn and upset the delicate balance. Caesar uses a much harsher image to describe the role of his sister in their friend-ship – 'the cement of our love / To keep it builded' (29-30). Compar-ing that 'love' to a castle under siege, he sternly warns Antony not to make her 'the ram to batter / The fortress of it' (30-1). The warning echoes what Enobarbus had said to Menas earlier: 'that which is the strength of their amity [that is, Octavia] shall prove the immediate author of their variance' (II.vi.130-2). A betrayal of Octavia will be considered a betrayal of Caesar himself. Antony replies with wounded dignity, 'Make me not offended / In your distrust', telling Caesar that there is not 'the least cause' for his 'fear' (33-6). But how are we to understand his reply? We already know that Antony, after first meeting Octavia, vowed that he 'will to Egypt' (II.iii.39). Is he lying here to save face? Or is he sincerely determined to make his marriage work? Caesar neither accepts nor rejects Antony's rebuke: 'I have said' is all he says.

The ambivalence of the scene is highlighted by the 'asides' of the on-lookers. Enobarbus wonders whether the 'cloud' in Caesar's face is a sign that he 'will weep'; in a horse that look would imply violence or bad temper, but Caesar, 'being a man', would not publicly display tears. Agrippa replies that Antony would never hesitate to weep; at Philippi, he openly wept over the bodies of friend (Julius Caesar) and enemy (Brutus) alike. Enobarbus counters that Antony was the *cause* of much of the grief that he then hypocritically wept over ('That year, indeed', Antony 'was troubled with a rheum' or running of the eyes). Caesar is too masculine, too 'Roman', to weep; Antony is too ready to use his weeping to impress others with his humanity (51-9).

In the end, Antony reaches out to embrace Caesar in farewell, but not in a way that will embarrass him: 'I'll wrestle with you in my strength of love' (62). The repetitions of 'farewell', as everyone leaves the stage, have an ominous ring. Caesar departs distrustful, Octavia unhappy, and Antony – perhaps sincere in his 'strength of love' for both Caesar and Octavia or perhaps just biding time until he returns to Egypt.

Act III, Scene iii

Summary
Cleopatra, now in a more moderate mood, quizzes the messenger who earlier had brought her the news of Antony's marriage. Interpreting his ambiguous description of Octavia in a way to give herself hope, she gives him gold and concludes that 'All may be well enough'.

Commentary
Could we imagine ourselves at the Globe theatre for the original performance of *Antony and Cleopatra*, the fanfare of trumpets following the last word of the last scene – Antony's 'Farewell!' to Rome and to Caesar – would still be sounding in our ears as Cleopatra and her attendants walk onto the stage at the beginning of this scene. Shakespeare's plays were performed without intervals or

scene changes; action was continuous. The flow of these two scenes, one into the other, forms an ironic commentary to Antony's assurance to Caesar that he has not 'the least cause' to 'distrust' him. Antony may be leaving with Octavia, but he *is* leaving Rome: and the reappearance of Cleopatra, after a long absence from the stage, justifies Caesar's concern and makes us doubt Antony's sincerity.

The last time we saw her (II.v), Cleopatra was stunned by the news of Antony's marriage and went off to grieve by herself. It is hard to believe, after the intervention of four eventful Roman scenes, that this new scene continues the action of II.v. In effect, these two Egyptian scenes frame the Roman scenes and leave the impression that events in both places are not consecutive, but simultaneous. While the alliance is being forged anew in Rome, Pompey put down, and Antony married, Cleopatra has been recovering from her initial shock; and now the wonderful resilience that marks her character reasserts itself. At the end of her last scene, she had sent Alexas to 'bid' the messenger return and give her a description of Octavia: 'Bring me word quickly', she ordered (II.v.115). The messenger now returns, clearly having learned his lesson well: he tells her what she wants to hear, or he answers her ambiguously. Cleopatra herself is the focus of comedy as she willingly deceives herself, but the comedy is welcome after the mistrust, intrigue, and political manoeuvring of the Roman scenes. Her humour does more, however, than provide comic relief; it charms us almost into allowing her the victory over Octavia. Yet Cleopatra is not without political judgement. When Alexas says, 'Herod of Jewry dare not look upon you / But when you are well pleased', she reminds him that, although she would have Herod's head, only Antony 'might command it' for her (3-6). There is always an element of uncertainty about Cleopatra: her feelings for Antony seem sincere, yet she also needs him politically.

Act III, Scene iv

Summary

In Athens, Antony tells Octavia that Caesar has warred against Pompey without having informed him, that he has read his will to the public (to curry favour with the populace), and that he has spoken disparagingly of Antony in public. Octavia urges Antony not to believe everything he hears. At her request, he allows her to return to Caesar as a mediator between them.

Commentary

This scene clearly shows how the political marriage of Antony and Octavia works: she is to moderate between him and Caesar. If the rumours of Caesar's violation of the treaty with Pompey and of his speaking 'scantly' of Antony in public are true (we cannot be sure at this point), it would appear that he has waited merely for Antony to be out of the way to pursue his goal of becoming sole emperor. It is Octavia's idea to return to Rome to reconcile them; for, if the quarrel stands, she loses, she says, either way: 'no midway / 'Twixt these extremes at all' (19-20). Antony warns her that, if she values his love, she must at the same time value his 'honour'; without that, he is not worthy of being her husband (22-4). And so it is for her 'honour', too, that she stand by him in this crisis. If one of them, brother or husband, is at fault, Octavia's 'best love' (21) cannot be given to them equally (34-6). Since he is conscious of having done no wrong to Caesar, his wife should not have to choose, or mediate, between them.

If it turns out that Caesar is at fault, then we have to ask whether he has not been using Octavia all along as part of a scheme to give him a good excuse to war against Antony. The rumour about Caesar's making his will and reading it 'To public ear' (4-5) is noteworthy: if it is true, his purpose is, transparently, to win the goodwill of the public, which tends to love Antony. (Caesar understands the fickleness of 'This common body', the mob; see I.iv.44-7). Were Antony to spurn Octavia, it would be easier to turn public opinion to Caesar's side.

Whatever Antony's feelings are about Octavia, and despite our knowing that he still harbours the wish to return to Egypt, her proposal to return to Rome obviously disturbs him. So far, he has made every effort to honour his marriage to Octavia and his bond with Caesar. Rome has no reason to fault him. His parting words to Octavia are blunt and rueful; he resents her not standing up for him. Meanwhile, he will prepare for war (26). From now on, the tension builds rapidly with each scene.

Act III, Scene v

Summary
In Antony's house in Athens, Eros and Enobarbus discuss Caesar's wars with Pompey and how, after having made use of Lepidus in them, Caesar has accused him of treachery. Lepidus now awaits death in prison. Eros reports Antony's anger not only at Caesar but also at Lepidus ('Fool Lepidus') for having given in so easily to Caesar. Meanwhile, Antony has summoned Enobarbus to him.

Commentary
Antony turns out to be right. The 'strange news' (2) of Caesar's renewed wars against Pompey, in violation of the treaty with the Triumvirate (II.vi), confirms the rumours of the preceding scene. The imprisonment of Lepidus, who now awaits death, on what look like contrived charges (7-13), has shattered the Triumvirate: Lepidus

had been the one factor keeping it together. And with Antony away from Rome, Caesar, in a ruthless grab for power, moves swiftly to 'possess' time (see II.vii.105), to gain the edge on Antony. War between the two seems inevitable. In a telling image, Enobarbus describes them as a 'pair of chaps' or jaws (with a pun on 'chaps' as 'fellows') that will grind against each other and in the process chew up many victims between them before they consume one another (14-16).

Some editors place the scene in Alexandria, but this is a mistake. Antony, for all his professed desire to return to Egypt, is still in Athens. He has not yet deserted Octavia; rather, she has left him – to mediate between her husband and her brother, of course; but, as Antony pointed out at the end of the last scene, only one of them can be at fault. Caesar, not Antony, is responsible for starting the war.

Act III, Scene vi

Summary
Caesar informs Agrippa and Maecenas that Antony has returned to Alexandria, where he has established Cleopatra as 'Absolute queen' of Egypt and proclaimed his sons 'the kings of kings' of the territories he has conquered. As he is explaining how he has answered Antony's charges against him, 'OCTAVIA *with her train*' enters; Caesar is appalled that she should come unannounced, without public ceremony befitting 'Caesar's sister'. When Octavia explains that she has come of her own 'free will' to mediate between her 'two friends / That [do] afflict each other', Caesar says that Antony granted her request readily so that he could hasten back to Cleopatra. In Egypt, Caesar tells her, Antony is amassing a great army.

Commentary
Antony has now played directly into Caesar's hands by returning to Egypt and thus giving Caesar the excuse to declare war against him. Caesar in this scene is a fascinating study of shrewdness, ruthlessness, and duplicity, in all of which Antony is deficient. Caesar sees himself as a man of destiny: 'But let determined things to destiny / Hold unbewailed their way' (84-5); at the same time he is determined to push his destiny along. It is easy to see why he will win: he has spies everywhere (62-63); he knows exactly what he wants; he takes advice from no one; and he thinks of everything. When Agrippa, for instance, urges him to answer Antony's accusations, he replies, ''Tis done already' (30-1); he does not wait for time to serve him. Earlier (III.iii), we saw how Cleopatra deceived herself in interpreting Octavia's features, but her self-deception served a psychological need. Whether Caesar believes everything that he says in this scene or whether he consciously twists everything to suit his purposes is

uncertain. His first words accusing Antony of 'Contemning [showing contempt for] Rome' are ironic in light of the previous scene where Antony was rightly angered by Caesar's breach of the treaty with Pompey and his high-handed imprisonment and sentencing of Lepidus – actions which to Antony's way of thinking betray any idea of Roman honour. Now Caesar is making himself out to be the honourable one, with Rome as his only concern. We learn, further-more, that he has kept Lepidus's treasure. No one, surely, who watches (or reads) this play will believe the reasons he has sent to Antony justifying his treatment of Lepidus: 'I have told him Lepidus was grown too cruel, / That he his high authority abused, / And did deserve his change' (32-4). Among the triumvirs, Lepidus was the most gentle, the most mild-mannered, the most concerned with keeping the Triumvirate united and in power. Even Caesar's pro-posals of peace are machiavellian: he purposely offers terms that he knows Antony will 'never yield to' (34-8). War, not peace, is his objective. When he needed Antony at his side to fight Pompey, things were different.

The unheralded entrance of Octavia with her small retinue ob-viously deprives Caesar of a great publicity stunt by preventing 'The ostentation of our love; which, left unshown, / Is often left unloved' (51-3). Love for him means the show of love. Octavia speaks the truth when she says that the fault is not Antony's; she came this way 'On my free will' (57; see Antony's last words to her at III.iv.36-8). But when she states that she had to beg Antony's 'pardon' to return to Rome, Caesar responds that her husband eagerly gave it so that he could hasten back to his 'whore' (57-67). Since Antony has, in fact, gone back to Egypt, Caesar's argument is hard to deny; yet, as we saw in the earlier scene, Antony reacted more in sorrow than in eagerness at Octavia's return to Rome. It seems obvious that Caesar is more concerned with portraying Antony as an adulterer than sorry for his sister. Not until some forty lines after her entrance does he 'Welcome' her (78). One cannot escape the impression that Octavia has served his purpose: she has become (did he plan it that way?) the instrument he needs to destroy the partnership with Antony.

Act III, Scene vii

Summary
To the dismay of Enobarbus, Cleopatra regards herself as an active participant in the war against Caesar. Contrary to his own military intelligence and advice of his officers, Antony, with Cleopatra's support, chooses to fight Caesar by sea, although he is better equipped for a land battle, only because Caesar has dared him to it. Caesar already is making great headway in his march towards Egypt.

Commentary

This scene is the first in a series that culminates in the naval battle between Caesar's and Antony's forces near Actium in 31 B.C. Cleopatra and Enobarbus enter in the midst of an argument, which she has already won. Enobarbus has been trying to convince Antony to forbid Cleopatra's presence at the forthcoming battle with Caesar, and she vows that she will avenge his interference (1). He regards her as a distraction for Antony, and is honest enough to tell her so (10-12). Her argument has a certain validity: since the war is 'denounced [declared] against us, why should not we / Be there in person?' (5-6). It is not as a woman or as Antony's lover that she will be present at the battle, but 'as president of my kingdom' and as a 'man' (17-18) – that is, as head of state.

What is at stake here, of course, is who will ultimately rule the Roman Empire, Caesar or Antony; but the scene reveals, more than anything else, the meaning of Antony's separation from Rome. He has now left that aspect of his activity which is Roman and has succumbed completely to Egypt. In choosing Cleopatra, he has thrown away 'The absolute soldiership' (41-2) which made him a success in Rome. Cleopatra has won him, but he has lost his judgement as a leader. It seems that Cleopatra has lost her judgement as well, for earlier she recognized that her greatness depended on him (see III.iii.4-6). His conduct in this scene, and in subsequent ones, is a denial of everything that made him a great statesman and general. His brusque, almost mechanical replies to his officers – 'By sea, by sea' (40) and 'I'll fight at sea' (48) – show how impervious he has become to reason. What he now needs is the cold, calculating mind of his opponent. Caesar is relentless in his single-minded pursuit of power, but Antony has done nothing so far and seems surprised by the swiftness of Caesar's advancing army. When Cleopatra officiously reminds him that 'Celerity is never more admired / Than by the negligent', Antony shrugs her criticism off as 'A good rebuke, / Which might have well become the best of men / To taunt at slackness' (25-7) – a compliment to Cleopatra that unwittingly echoes her resolve to join the battle as 'a man' (18) and recalls Agrippa's compliment to Antony as 'the best of men' (II.ii.130).

Enobarbus and the other officers blame Cleopatra for deluding Antony, but is it clear that she is at fault? Has she merely accepted *his* decision? Antony accepts Caesar's 'dare' or challenge to fight at sea when he must know that his army is better prepared and experienced to fight on land. His followers are still loyal to their 'noble emperor'; but even the lowliest soldier knows that his general's strategy is wrong (61-6). Why, then, does he accept such a 'dare' even after Caesar 'shakes off' Antony's offer to engage in 'single fight' because it serves 'not for his vantage' (29-40)? Our immediate impression is that Antony is foolhardy, Caesar merely practical. But there is another way to regard Antony's behaviour (the play constantly forces us to see characters and events from multiple perspectives). In choosing to fight at sea only because 'he dares us to 't' (29), Antony shows us that he lives by a code of honour that practical men like Caesar find laughable – a code that does not comprehend the for-swearing of oaths or treaties and certainly not the betrayal of friendships. That code is Roman, too; but it belongs to a time that antedates 'scarce-bearded Caesar'. Throughout the play Antony resents, does not even understand, the upstart ways of Caesar; but the conflict is more than one between generations: it entails different ways of giving meaning to life. Antony, like a medieval knight, belongs to an age of chivalry that, if not dead, is dying, giving way to a new, more practical and hard-boiled age (like the Renaissance?) of which Caesar is the representative man. Like the knights of old, Antony sees himself as both heroic warrior and heroic lover: his mission, to do honourable deeds for a woman who inspires him (see again his departing remarks to Cleopatra at I.iii.69-71). Of course, no one, probably not even Cleopatra, understands Antony's thinking or the code that animates his behaviour. Caesar's 'dare' is a challenge to Antony's old-fashioned sense of honour.

The scene ends with an image of time giving birth 'Each minute' (81) as events develop rapidly. Antony is unable to keep pace. Is there a suggestion in this scene that Antony has already half-accepted the inevitability of his defeat as a new era is about to overtake him?

Act III, Scene viii

Summary
Caesar orders Taurus, his lieutenant, not to do battle on land until 'we have done at sea', where he sees the advantage totally on his side.

Commentary
This brief scene at Caesar's headquarters comments eloquently on the previous scene. Caesar is self-confident, in charge, and certain of victory. He has carefully mapped out his battle plans, which he insists be followed as he has written them (4-5). In the earlier scene, Antony regarded a land battle as a last resort in case of failure at sea (III.vii.52-3). But here Caesar also sees the land battle as a last resort because he does not expect it to take place: he is placing his bet on the favourable outcome of the battle at sea ('Our fortune lies / Upon this jump', 5-6).

Act III, Scene ix

Summary
Antony offered Enobarbus to position their trooops ('on yon side o' the hill') where they will be able to assess Caesar's power at sea and know how to 'proceed accordingly'.

Commentary
Antony appears to recognize that Caesar's forces may surprise him by their strength at sea, as his officers had warned (III.vii), and he positions his 'squadrons' so that, if necessary, he will be ready to defend himself on land. It is clear that Caesar is taking the offensive, Antony the defensive position; but the scene shows Antony in a much more favourable light as a general than when we last saw him.

Act III, Scene x

Summary
The off-stage noise of a sea-battle is heard. Enobarbus, Scarus, and Canidius rush in, scarcely believing what they have just witnessed: in the midst of the battle, with no advantage on either side, possibly more on Antony's, Cleopatra suddenly took fright, and Antony – against all his 'Experience, manhood, honour' – fled after her. His 'ignorance' has lost him 'Kingdoms and provinces'. Scarus will wait and see what happens; but Canidius, Antony's lieutenant, will take his troops and horse, as six kings have done already, and desert to Caesar. Enobarbus, against 'reason', will still follow for a time the 'wounded chance of Antony'.

Commentary
Antony's defeat in this first battle against Caesar is swift. Shakespeare's open-air platform could not stage battles; off-stage noises and a few soldiers rushing in one door and out another were enough to suggest events. The conventions work to advantage here. Because we do not actually see Antony flee the battle (in which, ironically, given his supposed disadvantage at sea, he was doing very well, possibly winning), we are screened from his disgraceful action; Scarus, despite his anger and shock, suggests that some of Antony's grandeur remains (19). But the emphasis is not on Antony so much as on the psychological effect his flight has on his deserting followers (when we encounter him at the beginning of the next scene, we can better appreciate the depths of his anguish). Scarus is so beside himself that he can hardly speak straight; his description of what happened is a hodge-podge of mixed metaphors (Cleopatra as a 'nag' or horse that 'like a cow in June – / Hoists sails and flies', 10-15). Why she in fact hoisted sail and fled with her entire fleet of sixty ships

is a mystery that the play never answers. Earlier, she had told Enobarbus that she would 'Appear there for a man' (III.vii.18), and in the same scene Antony admired her manly 'rebuke' to him (III.vii.25-7). It is likely, however, that in the heat of the actual fighting, something she had never experienced before, she found herself not manly enough. In the next scene, she begs Antony, 'Forgive my fearful sails! I little thought / You would have followed' (III.xi.55-6). Indeed, why does he follow after her? Again, this is something of a mystery. Canidius says, 'Had our general / Been what he knew himself, it had gone well' (26-7). Antony knows himself as an 'absolute' soldier (see Enobarbus at III.vii.42), but his definition of that role comprehends more than the Roman: he considers himself Cleopatra's 'soldier, servant, making peace or war' as she chooses (I.iii.70-1). Cleopatra is his inspiration; without her, what meaning could the battle – or empire – have for him? No answer wholly satisfies.

The scene also marks the beginning of a conflict in Enobarbus which will develop later. Antony is now seen as no longer capable of leading an army, but Enobarbus will follow him for the time being 'though', as he says, 'my reason / Sits in the wind against me' (35-7).

Act III, Scene xi

Summary
Antony is despondent over his actions at Actium – for deserting the battle and following after Cleopatra. He broods on how he, a mature, experienced soldier, could have acted so shamefully before 'the young man' Caesar. He urges his followers to leave him and make their 'peace with Caesar'; he even offers them 'a ship / Laden with gold'. When Eros brings Cleopatra to comfort him, he at first blames her for his loss of honour; but he immediately admits that only he is to blame for making her his 'conqueror'. She asks his 'pardon', but he tells that there is nothing to forgive: one of her tears 'rates / All that is won and lost'. He has already sent their children's schoolmaster to negotiate the terms of peace with Caesar.

Commentary
Antony here is the very portrait of 'The noble ruin' described by Scarus in the last scene (III.x.19). As he *'sits down'* consumed by shame, Cleopatra herself is afraid to approach him, and does so only with prodding from Eros and her attendants: 'Well then, sustain me. O!' (45) For a while he seems unaware of her. The Antony she now sees is one whom she never imagined; and, when she does get through to him, we see a Cleopatra whom we could never have imagined: humble, frightened, tearful, almost at a loss for words. A hint of the old Cleopatra appears in her justification, 'I little thought /

You would have followed' (55-6); but an actress can interpret the line as one of bewilderment rather than of reproach.

Antony is a study in contrasts as blinding self-pity and and honest self-awareness war in his soul. Thoughts of suicide at the beginning of the scene (9-10) give way to stoical 'scorn' of 'Fortune' at the end (73-4). At the same time he thinks of his loyal followers with magnanimity. The 'ruin' of Antony lies in the first half of these contrasts: a man 'unqualitied with very shame' (44), that is, un-manned, emptied of those qualities that are indicative of his true self. This Antony is a man who, in his own word, has 'fled' himself (7). The 'noble' Antony, or the true one, lies in the second half of these contrasts: this Antony judges himself more severely than his severest critics judge him, and he is wonderful in admitting his mistakes.

By the end of the scene most of the contrasts seem favourably resolved with Antony's generous tribute to Cleopatra (69-71) and with his defiance of Fortune's 'blows' (73-4). We may recall another time when Antony also scorned such 'blows', in his retreat from Modena, and earned Caesar's unstinting admiration (I.iv.56-71). Antony does not give Cleopatra the 'pardon' for which she begs (61, 68); her tears convince him that he has made the right choice after all. Her love means everything to him, but the whole drift of the scene makes it painfully obvious that he also cannot live without the 'reputation' that only Rome can confer. The true Antony speaks when he tells Cleopatra that one of her tears 'rates / All that is won and lost' (69-71), but the equally true Antony speaks when he sits lamenting (49-50):

> I have offended reputation,
> A most unnoble swerving.

In Shakespeare's day, the word 'reputation' had a force that is almost lost today: it meant 'honour', and for a man to lose his 'reputation' meant losing the good of his name – without which he was nothing. In coming scenes Antony will again attempt to reconcile his 'reputa-tion' with his love for Cleopatra by being the soldier that she expects him to be. Although he has physically left Rome, he has not given up Rome: this is not a sentimental play in which the world is well lost for love.

Act III, Scene xii

Summary

Caesar receives Antony's ambassador, the schoolmaster, who con-veys his master's request 'to live in Egypt' or to live a 'private man in Athens'. The schoolmaster also brings a message from Cleopatra, who acknowledges Caesar's 'greatness' and 'craves' that she be allowed to remain as Queen of Egypt, with her crown descending to her heirs. To Antony's request, Caesar has 'no ears' at all; but he sends word to Cleopatra that, if she will rid Egypt of Antony or 'take his life there', she shall not be 'unheard'. Caesar commissions Thidias to go to Egypt to 'win Cleopatra' away 'From Antony' by eloquence and promises. He also wants Thidias to observe Antony's outward actions for what they reveal of his inward state since his recent disgrace.

Commentary

Antony, who once 'had superfluous kings for messengers' (5), now must resort to sending his children's schoolmaster (known as Euphronius in Plutarch). Caesar has no time for the schoolmaster's rhetoric and brusquely urges him to come to the point: 'Be 't so. Declare thine office' (7-10). To Antony he shows no generosity whatsoever; but his demand of Cleopatra to rid Egypt of Antony or 'take his life there' if she wishes to be heard (20-4) is politically and militarily realistic and perhaps a reminder of the insecurity this young man feels when he thinks of Antony – senior, experienced, and almost worshipped by much of the world.

The 'cunning' that Caesar asks Thidias to use on his mission (31) is characteristic of Caesar himself as he ambiguously holds out hope to Cleopatra: 'if she perform' his request regarding Antony, he tells the schoolmaster, 'She shall not sue unheard' (23-4); he is careful not to promise that he will grant her 'desire' to remain Queen of Egypt and pass the crown on to her heirs. Since Caesar shares the Roman view of Cleopatra as a 'whore' (see III.vi.66-7), it is not surprising that he is convinced that she can be purchased. What may be surprising is his contempt for women in general: he is sure that even Rome's Vestal Virgins, priestesses renowned for their chastity and incorruptibility, could similarly be bought (29-31). One wonders about his true feelings for his sister, whom he was willing to use as a political pawn. That Cleopatra could love Antony does not strike him as a possibility, for he seems not even to know what love is.

Act III, Scene xiii

Summary

Antony tells Cleopatra the results of his embassy to Caesar. He is disconsolate as he wonders how someone so inexperienced in warfare, still in 'the rose / Of youth', 'the boy Caesar', has been able to conquer him; he cannot help dwelling on the person that he was and the person that he has now become. In desperation, to prove his worth, he contemplates challenging Caesar to a duel. After he leaves, Cleopatra receives Caesar's ambassador, Thidias, who tries to alien-

ate her from Antony by telling her that Caesar knows she 'embraced
not Antony / As you did love, but as you feared him'. She answers
him ambiguously, but allows him to kiss her hand – at which point
Antony enters, becomes outraged at both of them, and orders
Thidias whipped. He is soon 'satisfied', however, that Cleopatra
loves him, and they leave together to celebrate her birthday. Enobarbus now begins to think seriously of deserting Antony.

Commentary
Cleopatra and Enobarbus are in the middle of a conversation when
the scene begins. Cleopatra had told Antony that she 'little thought /
You would have followed' (III.xi.55-6); but apparently she has been
wondering whether she was to blame for Antony's defeat at Actium.
Enobarbus assures her that the fault was Antony's only, for he
allowed his 'will' and the 'itch of his affection' or sexual desires to
overcome 'reason'. Antony, in his view, behaved shamefully when he
fled and left 'his navy gazing', for he was the 'merèd question' or sole
reason for the battle in the first place (1-12). Seemingly relieved,
Cleopatra says nothing; and, when Antony and his ambassador enter,
she puts an end to the discussion.

The ambassador has relayed Caesar's 'answer' (see III.xii.19-24) to
Antony but not yet to Cleopatra; and so when Antony bitterly tells
her that 'the boy Caesar' 'will fill thy wishes to the brim / With
principalities' if she sends him 'this grizzled head', she does not know
what he is talking about: 'That head, my lord?' (17-19). Caesar's
'youth' obsesses Antony, and in the speech that follows (20-8), he is
again full of self-pity. Does Antony fear Caesar? After his defeat, he
berated himself for his 'fear and doting', as well as for his 'rashness'
(III.xi.13-15). Was he rash in fleeing or in fighting Caesar at sea on
Caesar's 'dare', and was Cleopatra's defection a good excuse for him
to flee? We are on murky grounds here, and nothing in the play will
give us a clear answer. Antony now tries to persuade himself that
Caesar's advantage lies not in personal superiority but in the greater
'coins, ships, legions' at his disposal. Although it is true that he
continually underestimates Caesar's political genius, what matters
most in Antony's code of behaviour is personal worth; and he cannot
see that his younger rival has in any 'particular' way distinguished
himself. To prove to the world who is the worthier of the two, he now
dares Caesar to a duel with him, 'sword against sword' (20-8).
Enobarbus realizes that Caesar, with great armies at his command
('High-battled'), is not likely to stake all his gains on a mere
sword-fight (28-36). He sees *both* Caesar and Cleopatra as having
'subdued' Antony's judgement, and his reason tells him that to
continue serving a fool is not loyalty but mere foolishness. Nevertheless, he is not quite ready to desert, for he recognizes that it is nobler
to 'follow with allegiance a fallen lord' and earn 'a place i' the story'

(41-6). The last phrase is ambiguous, referring to a place in history or in the play itself. For the audience, it creates suspense about Enobarbus's future actions.

After Antony has left, Caesar's ambassador, Thidias, enters. Cleopatra shrewdly observes that he appears before her without the 'ceremony' that her position should normally command (38). Although she does not say so, her vague responses to him in the dialogue that follows reveal that she can see by his disrespect what is in store for her. Neither side gives in very much or says anything too specific. Cleopatra's short replies can be interpreted seriously or ironically: they really say nothing; they give the impression that she is playing for time. But Enobarbus fails to see how cleverly she is handling Thidias. When she tells Thidias that her 'honour was not yielded' to Antony, 'But conquered merely' (61-2), Enobarbus is so outraged that he rushes off to 'ask Antony' about that; but most of us will understand that, indeed, she did not yield to Antony but rather was swept off her feet by him. None of the Romans seems to understand passion; to them it is just an 'itch of . . . affection'.

Caesar has underestimated Cleopatra, and so have his ambassador and Enobarbus. No one really knows her, and in what follows even Antony fails to understand her. Cleopatra is obviously stunned by his tirade against her (105-157) after he sees her offering her hand to Thidias for a kiss. 'Not know me yet?', she asks in bewilderment (157). She has played with Thidias (and, by implication, with Caesar), but in holding out her hand for a kiss she has not played *into* his hands at all. For a while all she can do is let Antony's rage take its course. 'Wherefore is this?' she asks (122), and 'Have you done yet?' (153). In ordering Thidias to be whipped, Antony is acting like a powerful man; but a secure man would not have yielded to the impulse. Yet, he deserves to be treated better than a lackey by Caesar's own servant (86-8); whatever his condition now, he is, as he says, 'Antony yet' (93). Thidias, of course, takes his cue from Caesar; he writes Antony off completely.

Antony, then, does not 'know' Cleopatra (and, in fact, he never will; neither will we); but her impassioned denial (158-67) that she has ever been 'Cold-hearted' satisfies him and even restores the will to oppose Caesar's siege of Alexandria (167-79). He is 'satisfied' (167) as quickly now as he was when she asked 'pardon' (III.xi.68-71); he needs to believe her.

Before the scene is over, Antony says, 'Come, / Let's have one other gaudy night' (182-3). We marvel at the way Antony's natural buoyancy reasserts itself in the midst of his despair. But there is a marked difference between this occasion and a much earlier one when he had said to Cleopatra, 'And all alone / Tonight we'll wander through the streets and note / The qualities of people' (I.i.52-4). Then he truly was carefree, but now desperation colours his lively spirits.

In this scene, Antony seems to suggest that they live for one more night, for tomorrow will be the end. The 'child o' the time' (II.vii.104) now finds that time is not his forever. Enobarbus interprets Antony's self-summons to courage as noisy boasting to frighten fear away, and he decides 'to leave him' (195-201) – to take himself out of 'the story'. He is both right and wrong to do so. 'Valour' without 'reason' or discretion may be the way to suicide, as he says (199-200), but he has yet to discover which is preferable: Antony's warm, passionate, impulsive nature or the coldly calculating self-interest of Caesar.

Act IV, Scene i

Summary
A letter from Antony angers Caesar, but at the same time he laughs 'at his challenge' to 'personal combat': 'I have many other ways to die', he says. Maecenas sees Antony's rage as a sign of a defeated man and urges Caesar to strike at this opportune moment. Caesar notes that the number of Antony's deserters within his own army would be enough to defeat 'Poor Antony!'

Commentary
As Enobarbus had predicted, Caesar finds Antony's challenge simply absurd; he is convinced that his own army will defeat Antony's in one 'last' battle 'tomorrow' (10-12). In contrast to the Antony of the preceding scene, Caesar's only hint of anger is his response of 'old ruffian' (4) to Antony's taunt of 'boy'; otherwise, he does not let 'valour' or his feelings '[prey] on reason' or, as Maecenas says, allow his 'anger' to put him off 'guard' (9-10). Even ordering a 'feast' for his troops is no generous impulse but a calculated move to increase their zest for the next day's fighting; besides, 'they have earned the waste' (14-16) or what he considers a wasteful or needless expenditure of supplies and money. A sound idea, but without heart. Caesar's final words, 'Poor Antony!' are perhaps a mixture of condescension and pity for a soldier whom he once admired.

Act IV, Scene ii

Summary
Antony seems surprised that Caesar has not accepted his challenge to fight a duel, but Enobarbus says,that Caesar would be foolish to do so when his troops outnumber Antony's twenty to one. Like Caesar, Antony also sees tomorrow as crucial. He summons his 'household servants' to thank them for their loyal service, and orders a 'bounteous' meal for the evening. Everyone weeps, including the cynical Enobarbus, when Antony tells them that this may be their last night

together. Cleopatra does not understand what he is up to. When Enobarbus upbraids him for making him and the others 'onion-eyed', Antony turns everything into a joke, saying that he expects to win tomorrow's battle.

Commentary

What are we to make of Antony in this scene? Even Cleopatra fails to understand him: twice she has to ask Enobarbus, 'What means this?' (13) and 'What does he mean?' (23); Enobarbus gives the cynical answer: 'To make his followers weep' (24; compare what he has to say on Antony's weeping at III.ii.57-9). We may be tempted to accuse Antony of playing upon the emotions of his followers; but even Enobarbus finds himself weeping (35-6). If our first impression here is that Antony is insincere, other moments in the play confirm his generous, open-hearted, and forgiving nature. We should note how his generosity and *direct* expression of gratitude dramatically contrast with the behaviour of Caesar in the preceding scene. This scene underscores again, late in the play, the human qualities that have made Antony universally admired; and it makes clearer the tumult of feelings that have been there from the beginning but that now, thanks to the urgency of the situation, tumble out of him with more intensity.

Antony's expectation of victory on the morrow does smack of wishful thinking, especially in light of Caesar's certainty. Antony's final lines (36-45), although high-spirited, contain hints of his desperation: 'Let's to supper, come, / And drown consideration'. He seems to 'Know' (41) or sense that he cannot be the winner.

Act IV, Scene iii

Summary

Several of Antony's guards discuss the battle to take place next day. Suddenly, they hear from '*under the stage*' (original First Folio direction) the 'strange' music of 'hautboys' (oboes). They are uncertain of its meaning, except for one soldier, who interprets it as a sign that 'the god Hercules, whom Antony loved, / Now leaves him'. They follow the music, as far as their posting allows, to see how it will cease.

Commentary

In contrast to the preceding scene where Antony rouses his 'household servants' with the expectation of 'victorious life' in tomorrow's battle, the low, dark tones of the 'hautboys' create an atmosphere of foreboding. The anonymity of Antony's loyal guards suggests that their uneasiness is felt throughout the army. Like the audience itself, these soldiers are uncertain about what the music means. One soldier hesitantly says, 'It signs well, does it not?' Another answers simply, 'No' (13). The second soldier who claims that it signals the departure of Antony's 'loved' god Hercules makes an impression because he is so definite. At this moment, atmosphere counts more than meaning.

At I.iii.84, Cleopatra, mockingly, calls Antony 'this Herculean Roman'. Plutarch writes that Antony was said to be descended from Hercules but that on this particular night it was the god Bacchus (see II.vii.117-22 and the commentary), to whom Antony was singularly devoted, who forsook him. Shakespeare deliberately has changed Bacchus to Hercules, a hero of enormous strength and courage, but one who also had to undergo extraordinary agony and suffering as a test of his heroism.

Act IV, Scene iv

Summary

The morning of the great battle. Cleopatra urges Antony to 'Sleep a little', but he calls for Eros to help him with his armour. Cleopatra insists on arming him; and, although she really does not know what she is doing, Antony enjoys and praises her efforts. At the sound of trumpets flourishing, Antony's captains and soldiers greet him. Without elaborate ceremony (or 'mechanic compliment'), he gives Cleopatra a straightforward 'soldier's kiss' and departs. Seeing him go forth so 'gallantly', Cleopatra wishes that 'he and Caesar might / Determine this great war in single fight!': she is certain who would win in that case.

Commentary

This scene is a welcome interlude in the series of ominously tense scenes, especially the immediately preceding one, building up to the decisive battle. Antony and Cleopatra are happier than in any other previous scene, for they are acting out roles which completely fulfil them: Antony as the complete soldier preparing for the 'business that we love' (20) and Cleopatra as the 'armourer of [his] heart' (7). Cleopatra has learned her lesson: she makes no demands to be a direct participant in 'this great war' (37) but, like the 'lady' of medieval romantic literature, she proudly sees her knight in shining armour off to do battle for her and win honour for himself. She now helps Antony with his armour, in contrast to the time when she boasted of their exchanging roles, when she 'put my tires [head-dresses] and mantles on him, whilst / I wore his sword Philippan' (II.v.22-3). Nevertheless, the good feeling in this scene is tempered by its resemblance to the so-called 'false-dawn' in classical tragedy when hope is held out to the hero before he is finally struck down. At the end of the scene, even Cleopatra has a moment of doubt: seeing

Antony depart so 'gallantly', she feels sure that he could win easily 'in single fight' with Caesar; but her spirits momentarily give way to mingled hope and resignation at the thought of 'this great war' and Caesar's enormous advantages: 'Well, on' (36-8).

Act IV, Scene v

Summary
A soldier informs Antony that Enobarbus has deserted him and gone over to Caesar, leaving behind 'his chests and treasure'. Antony directs Eros to send these to Enobarbus at once and to write a letter, which he will sign, bidding Enobarbus 'gentle adieus and greetings'. He does not blame Enobarbus or the other deserters but only himself, aware that his own 'fortunes have / Corrupted honest men!'

Commentary
Cleopatra has just seen Antony going forth to battle 'gallantly'. In this next scene, Antony could not appear more 'gallant' in another sense – in generosity of spirit. When he meets the soldier who tells him of Enobarbus's desertion, Antony admits that he wished he had listened earlier to his soldiers and fought on land (2-3). When not acting impulsively, Antony always seems capable of confronting himself. The desertion of Enobarbus, his trusted adviser and confidant, is one of his lowest moments; but his noble reaction reflects the serenity of his mood. Assured of Cleopatra's love, he can be honest with himself and take on the world. Rage and self-pity were his reactions to her desertion at Actium; to Enobarbus's desertion he reacts with dignity and sadness. His last word in the scene – 'Enobarbus!' – is a cry from the heart, but his awareness of how much his 'fortunes' have harmed his followers is not coupled with regret for having chosen Cleopatra.

Act IV, Scene vi

Summary
Caesar orders the start of the battle and asks that Antony 'be took alive'. A messenger announces that Antony has come into the field, and Caesar orders that those who deserted from Antony should be placed in the front lines to demoralise his opponent. Left alone, Enobarbus mournfully observes that he has 'done ill' to desert Antony; he sees how Caesar shows 'No honourable trust' in the deserters. One of Caesar's soldiers reports to Enobarbus that Antony has sent back his treasure. Enobarbus is so overcome with grief by this magnanimity that he contemplates suicide.

Commentary

This scene brings out the sharpest contrast between Caesar and Antony simply as human beings. Whereas Caesar is mistrustful, petty, and ungrateful, Antony is open-hearted, generous, and forgiving. Although it would appear from the initial stage direction – '*Enter* AGRIPPA *and* CAESAR, *with* ENOBARBUS *and* DOLABELLA' – that Enobarbus has Caesar's trust, as he comes to know Caesar better, he has 'joy no more' (20) in what he has done. The juxtaposition of this scene with the last, in which we hear of his desertion, shows how quickly he feels the consequences. What is more important is that he realises Caesar's true nature even *before* he learns of Antony's magnificent gesture in returning his treasure and goods. That Caesar's own soldier says of Antony, 'Your emperor / Continues still a Jove' makes Enobarbus feel 'alone the villain of the earth' (28-30).

Militarily and politically, Enobarbus has made the right decision to abandon Antony, but what does this scene say of his earlier praise of 'reason' (as at III.xiii.199) and of Roman morality in general? The Romans have always been quick to call Cleopatra a 'whore' (see III.vi.67, for instance), but in a sense the 'rational' Enobarbus has also 'whored'; knowing that he has done so is his tragedy. His new-found knowledge makes us reflect on his earlier cynical comments and suspect that they were not always accurate interpretations of Antony's actions.

Act IV, Scene vii

Summary

Caesar's army is in retreat. Scarus, one of Antony's soldiers, despite being wounded, is eager to get back into battle and finish the job. Antony commends him for his 'valour'.

Commentary

To Agrippa's surprise (and maybe ours, too), Antony is winning. In the previous scene, Caesar believed that Antony was isolated, that he would 'spend his fury / Upon himself' when confronted by his deserters in Caesar's front rank (IV.vi.9-11); but he had not figured on the loyalty that Antony still commands. Antony's first words to Scarus show why his men are still attracted to him: 'Thou bleed 'st apace' (6) – Scarus's wounds concern him more than anything else at this moment. Unlike Enobarbus, Scarus offers Antony 'sprightly comfort' (15), and like his 'brave emperor' (4; note how frequently Antony's status is played upon in this sequence of scenes) he is himself 'sprightly'.

Act IV, Scene viii

Summary
Antony's army has driven Caesar back 'to his camp'. Antony sends a messenger to inform Cleopatra of the valiant deeds performed; while he awaits her, he thanks his soldiers for their loyalty. Each man, he says, fought as if the cause were his own, not just Antony's. When Cleopatra appears, Antony commends Scarus to her, and she promises him 'An armour all of gold'. Antony then calls for trumpeters to proclaim a celebration march through Alexandria.

Commentary
Cleopatra has armed Antony for battle (IV.iv), and now he returns victorious. The exuberance of the scene is genuine, but is Antony deluding himself? His behaviour may remind us of the last hundred days of Napoleon, after his return from exile and before his final defeat. This scene is the subject of more detailed critical analysis in Chapter 5, 'Specimen Passage and Commentary'.

Act IV, Scene ix

Summary
Caesar's sentries, keeping watch on a hushed, moonlit night before the next day's battle, overhear the grieving Enobarbus lamenting his 'infamous' desertion of Antony. After a while, they think he has fallen asleep, maybe fainted; but they discover instead that the 'hand of death' has touched him.

Commentary
Antony's exciting return, unharmed, 'from / The world's great snare' is followed by the quiet, melancholy scene of Enobarbus's death. Even before Antony's victory, Enobarbus regretted his decision to follow Caesar (IV.vi). His own reason has convinced him of Antony's unreason, which did not deserve his loyalty; in Caesar's camp, however, he quickly realized Antony's nobility (which all the scenes since his defeat at Actium have emphasised): 'O Antony,/ Nobler than my revolt is infamous' (18-19). As a 'master-leaver' (22), a servant who deserts his master, Enobarbus is guilty of overturning the social order; but, more seriously, he has become a 'fugitive' (22) even from himself, by his choice of reason, judgement and discretion over loyalty and affection: he has fled from himself – his Egyptian half? (Compare Antony when he says, after his defeat at Actium, 'I have fled myself' – his Roman self; III.xi.7). Enobarbus's final words, 'O Antony! O Antony!' recall Antony's cry of 'Enobarbus!' (IV.v.17) when he hears of his friend's desertion. Both really need the other: Antony for Enobarbus's discretion, Enobarbus for Antony's affection.

The manner of Enobarbus's death is ambiguous. It is not clear that he has committed suicide. When Cleopatra, after her desertion of Antony at Actium, asked him, 'What shall we do, Enobarbus?', he replied, 'Think, and die' (III.xiii.1). He has now fulfilled his own prophecy, dying of a broken heart when he could bear life no longer.

Moonlight, symbolic of the transitory nature of this world, and the poisonous night air are the images of this scene (7, 11-12). The quiet ('demure'), mournful rolling of drums contrasts with the brazen trumpets that ended the previous scene.

Act IV, Scene x

Summary
Antony tells Scarus that Caesar, having failed on land, is preparing for another battle at sea. Antony is willing to fight him anywhere, and so gives 'order for sea'.

Commentary
We know that Antony's forces are superior on land, but his sense of honour dictates that he meet Caesar anywhere, even 'i 'the fire or i' the air'; his bravery may seem more like bravado, but at this point his transcendent mood from IV.viii still prevails: he seems indifferent to the material universe. The imagery of the play so far has emphasized water and earth, especially the image of the Nile's overflow and its muddy banks; the references to fire and air in this scene mark a change.

Act IV, Scene xi

Summary
Caesar, meanwhile, orders his forces to be prepared to fight by land and to maintain the positions they already hold, unless they are attacked, while Antony is committing 'his best force' to sea.

Commentary
This four-line scene is enough to show us how carefully Caesar plots his strategy in contrast to Antony's lack of planning. Antony believes that Caesar is planning another sea-battle; but Caesar actually is hoping to decoy Antony's 'best' soldiers away from land, where they have been winning, and return the 'best advantage' to himself.

Act IV, Scene xii

Summary
Off-stage, the noise '*as at a sea fight*' is heard. Antony goes to check whether the battle has actually begun. Scarus observes that Antony is by turns 'valiant' and 'dejected', full of 'hope and fear'. Antony

returns, furious that his fleet has 'yielded to the foe'; he believes
Cleopatra has betrayed him. Cleopatra arrives and is so perplexed by
his great rage that she leaves at once. Savagely, he threatens that
'The witch', as he now calls her, 'shall die'.

Commentary

Only the four-line scene with Caesar separates an Antony confident
that he can fight Caesar anywhere from an Antony in final defeat.
'Fortune and Antony part here' (19) is one of the most powerful of
the play's images of dissolving, melting, o'erflowing: of hearts that
followed Antony like spaniels but now 'do discandy' or 'melt their
sweets / On blossoming Caesar' (20-3). Ironically, Cleopatra has
herself used the word 'discandying' earlier (III.xiii.165) when she
invoked a curse upon herself if her love for Antony proved 'Cold-
hearted'. Antony now curses her. Obviously remembering Caesar's
offer to hear her wishes for retaining the crown of Egypt if she
banishes Antony or kills him (III.xii.20-4), Antony is now convinced
that 'This foul Egyptian hath betrayèd me' (10). For the first time in
the play he joins the other Romans in calling her 'whore' (13) and
'gypsy' (28). But can we be sure that she has betrayèd him? It is
Antony's own fleet that 'hath yielded to the foe' (11). There may be a
clue in what follows (43-7). Antony calls upon his ancestor Alcides,
or Hercules, to 'teach' him not human anger but a heroic 'rage'
worthy of him; only the fury of Hercules can 'subdue' Antony's
'worthiest self'. There is now no place for self-pity or despair as there
was after Actium. 'The shirt of Nessus' is now 'upon' him: Nessus was
the centaur whom Hercules mortally wounded with a poisoned arrow
when he tried to rape Deianira, Hercules's wife. As he lay dying,
Nessus told Deianira that his blood-soaked shirt would prove a charm
to regain Hercules's love, but instead it killed him. (In the throes of
pain caused by the poison from Nessus's blood, Hercules hurled
Lichas, the servant who brought him the shirt, into the air – lodged
'Lichas on the horns o' the moon'.) But the irony is that Deianira sent
the shirt in good faith; she did not betray Hercules. When she learned
the effect of her gift, she killed herself. Could this allusion be
Shakespeare's way of letting us know that Cleopatra is not to blame?
Her single line in the scene – 'Why is my lord enraged against his
love?' (31) – may be one of perplexity rather than a hypocritical
expression of comfort, as some critics have read it.

Earlier in the scene, Antony invokes the 'sun', whose 'uprise' he
'shall...see no more' (18), and in doing so he recalls for us the time,
only a short while ago, when he called Cleopatra his 'day o' the
world' (IV.viii.13). Now he is ready to kill her. The fury of Hercules
has taken hold of him.

Act IV, Scene xiii

Summary
Cleopatra, puzzled by Antony's rage, follows Charmian's advice to
lock herself in her monument (the tomb prepared for her death) and
to send the eunuch Mardian to tell Antony that she is dead.

Commentary
Each separation of Antony and Cleopatra seems more violent than
the last, each reconciliation more intense. Antony's madness, the
violence of his fury, puzzles more than angers her. Charmian
associates his present state with his 'greatness going off' (6), more
painful to Antony than the 'parting' of the 'soul and body' at death
(5-6). The question for Cleopatra now is how to get him back; she
responds with an act of desperation.

Act IV, Scene xiv

Summary
As Antony compares himself to the changing shapes of clouds at
nightfall, his trusty servant Eros stands by and weeps. Still believing
that Cleopatra has betrayed him, Antony says that there is nothing
left but to take his own life ('Ourselves to end ourselves'). Mardian
announces Cleopatra's 'death', saying that her last words were
'Antony! Most noble Antony!' Antony feels overwhelming remorse
for having misjudged her, and promises to 'o'ertake' her and 'Weep'
for his pardon. He asks Eros to fulfil a promise made long ago when
Antony had freed him from slavery – that he would take Antony's
life at a moment of disgrace. Eros is reluctant, but is persuaded when
Antony points out that death is preferable to being led in triumph
behind Caesar in Rome. While Antony turns his back at Eros's
request, Eros kills himself. Shamed by his servant's 'nobleness',
Antony tries to take his own life by falling on his sword but succeeds
only in wounding himself. He calls for his guards and requests of any
'that loves me strike me dead', but none is willing. Diomedes rushes
in with an urgent message from Cleopatra that she had feigned
suicide to subdue Antony's rage but now has a 'prophesying fear' that
he might take his own life. Antony orders his guards to carry him to
Cleopatra.

Commentary
A point to observe is Antony's resolve to die even before he hears of
Cleopatra's 'death'. Her deceit is not the cause of his suicide. A great
change has come over Antony since we last saw him. The 'rage' of
Hercules has spent itself; it has subdued his 'worthiest self'

(IV.xii.47), and a kind of peace has descended upon him. Antony has never in the play been given to meditating, but here he is sombre and reflective. His comparison of himself to the ever-changing clouds (2-14) reminds us of images of dissolution throughout the play: Antony now feels that he no longer has any 'visible shape' (14) or identity. Both Rome and Egypt have disappointed him. He is less disappointed than perplexed by Cleopatra, 'Whose heart I thought I had, for she had mine' (16); for her he 'made these wars' (15), recalling for us the time that he left Egypt to return to Rome *only* as her 'soldier, servant, making peace or war / As thou affects' (I.iii.69-71). Now he has neither occupation, for, as he says, 'She has robbed me of my sword' (23).

The news of her 'death', however, convinces Antony that Cleopatra had always loved him, and his projected suicide becomes a whole action, no longer prompted by disappointment. As he calls Eros to help him, his servant's name becomes associated with Eros or Cupid, the god of love: 'Eros! – I come, my queen – Eros! – Stay for me' (50). In his new mood, Antony harbours no illusions about Cleopatra, but he feels no resentment towards her either. Her death, however, gives new meaning to his reflection that he is 'No more a soldier' (42): without her, his 'royal occupation' (see IV.iv.17) is gone.

Suicide is not only Antony's way of rejoining Cleopatra 'Where souls do couch on flowers' (51); it brings together for him the images of Rome and Egypt. 'Since Cleopatra died', he says, 'I have lived in such dishonour that the gods / Detest my baseness' (55-7). The one means that he has left to reclaim the Roman virtue that has meant the most to him is suicide: by taking his own life he can show Caesar, as Cleopatra has done before him, that 'I am conqueror of myself' (60-2) and put his own 'Nobleness in record' (99). Just before he falls on his sword, he thinks of Cleopatra as both wife (Roman) and lover (Egyptian): 'But I will be / A bridegroom in my death, and run into 't / As to a lover's bed' (99-101). His private and public lives become one at the moment of death. But Cleopatra is alive after all! That Antony has come through his Herculean test, his agony and suffering, to a new understanding is proved by his reaction to the news: he does not blame her for her deception; he says nothing except to order his guards to take him to her. Everything that Cleopatra does has always been a mystery to him, part of her 'infinite variety'; he calmly accepts that.

Antony's botched suicide is less than heroic. Nevertheless, the poetry brings before us an Antony larger, more glorious than the sorry figure lying wounded on the stage. Decretas brutally says that Antony's sword will gain him a place with Caesar (111-13). But the scene impresses us more with the loyalty and devotion of Antony's followers: Eros, who kills himself rather than 'My dear master, / My captain, and my emperor' (89-90), and the anonymous guards whom Antony's attempted suicide has made eloquent ('The star is fallen.' / 'And time is at her period', 106-7). Such language raises Antony above the moralizing judgements of Rome's 'common liar' (I.i.60).

Act IV, Scene xv

Summary

Cleopatra at her tomb refuses comfort. Diomedes confirms her worst fear, that Antony has attempted suicide and is near death. Guards carry Antony in; and he is heaved aloft to the top of the monument because Cleopatra, fearing capture by Caesar, will not descend from it. Even as he is dying, Antony bids her to seek safety with Caesar and trust only Caesar's officer Proculeius; but she replies that honour and safety 'do not go together' with Caesar. Antony makes a moving farewell speech in which he defends his suicide as 'a Roman, by a Roman / Valiantly vanquished' and dies in Cleopatra's arms. Life without Antony holds nothing for her, and she vows to take her own life 'after the high Roman fashion' once she has buried Antony. She and her attendants bear his body away.

Commentary

Even before she hears of Antony's suicide, Cleopatra senses that she will never leave her monument. Death holds no terror for her, and she welcomes 'All strange and terrible events' but 'no comforts' for her grief (1-4). Just as Antony's greatness had demanded from him a Herculean 'rage' (IV.xii.43-4), so Cleopatra's 'size of sorrow' must be 'Proportioned' to Antony's greatness (and possibly to her own guilt at having tempted him 'too far'); nothing less will do (4-6). Some critics think that she is merely play-acting, but we should remember that both she and Antony are conscious of their roles as great public figures; unlike Caesar, whose self-control masks any unmanly show of emotion, they 'proportion' their feelings to their stature. Their spontaneous display of feelings is what makes them so compelling to their followers, as well as to audiences; they sum up the 'infinite variety' of human emotions, whereas Caesar, for all his worldly success, seems a lesser human being.

What is remarkable about their last moments together is the absence of recriminations. As mature lovers they have never harboured illusions about one another. Though her grief is obviously sincere, even at this final moment in Antony's life Cleopatra will not come down to give him one last kiss; instead, with great difficulty ('A heavy sight!', 40) and in a race with time, she and her women lift him up to her (18-40). Antony feels neither resentment nor betrayal, and he also feels no regrets: the 'miserable change now at my end' is of no account when measured against his 'former fortunes' (51-3). His life has been devoted to heroic achievement, and his 'nobleness in record' (IV.xiv.99) speaks for itself: his suicide restores his 'reputation' as 'the greatest prince o' the world, / The noblest' (54-5). Antony is not boasting here but speaks as one whose recent agony and suffering equip him to see life steadily and whole. This is the voice of a man already beyond 'The varying shore o' the world' (11). Antony has always been generous, but never more so than here: his final thoughts are about Cleopatra's 'honour' and 'safety' (45-6). His 'former fortunes' are recalled as much to comfort Cleopatra as to set the record straight. To the end, Antony loves without regret, and yet in death he achieves greatness as a Roman. Dying in Cleopatra's arms, he reconciles the two worlds, Rome and Egypt, as in life he could not. The death of Enobarbus was a sad affair, almost unnoticed in a ditch on a dark night; it was the price he had to pay for denying the passionate side of his humanity. Antony's death, in contrast, movingly restores the full man. But, as Cleopatra says, 'woe 'tis so!' (17).

A series of impressive speeches marks the death of Antony, beginning with the eloquence of his anonymous guards (IV.xiv.106-7). But Cleopatra's are the most eloquent, beginning with her great image of dissolution: 'The crown o' the earth doth melt' (63). The images she evokes are simultaneously martial and erotic (Roman and Egyptian), for Antony the soldier and the lover: 'O, withered is the garland of the war, / The soldier's pole is fall'n' (64-6). 'The odds is gone', she says (66), for Antony had set the standard for measuring greatness: the world has now seen the last of his type; the new standard is Caesar, and what will be measured is success, not greatness. For a while, grief seems to strike her senseless (68-70).

By the end of the scene, there is no denying Cleopatra's 'resolution' (91) to take her own life. The word 'Roman' is no longer distasteful to her (see I.ii.83 for her reaction to Antony's 'Roman thought') – as if Antony's death brings home to her how much his greatness was inseparable from his 'Romanness'. She vows to end her life in a manner appropriate to Antony – 'what's brave, what's noble,...after the high Roman fashion' (86-7). In her grief, Cleopatra senses her common humanity – 'No more but e'en a woman', responding to her loss as would the lowliest milkmaid (72-4). But the sight of her grieving attendants and Antony's grieving guards reminds her that she is Queen of Egypt, and with royal composure she puts aside her sorrow to comfort them (82-8). As for herself, she will 'make death proud to take us'. The scene ends with the moving sight of Cleopatra and her attendants 'bearing off ANTONY'S body' (original stage direction). Royal dignity bows before the simple task of caring for the dead.

52

Act V, Scene i

Summary
Caesar orders Dolabella to go bid Antony to surrender. Immediately
thereafter, Decretas arrives '*with the sword of Antony*' and shocks
Caesar with the news of Antony's suicide. Even though he had
wished for Antony's destruction, 'Caesar is touched' by the news but
at the same time recognizes that the two of them could not have
shared the rule of empire together. An Egyptian brings word that
Cleopatra awaits Caesar's 'instruction', and Caesar assures him 'How
honourable and how kindly we / Determine for her'. Caesar then
sends his own officer, Proculeius, to her under the pretext of
confirming his promise of gentle treatment but in reality to watch
over her lest she also commit suicide and deprive him of exhibiting
her in his Roman triumph.

Commentary
Cleopatra's response to Antony's death is now followed by Caesar's.
Caesar, too, lends majesty to the event by his uncharacteristically
charitable reaction. From the first, he has shown a grudging admiration for the older, more renowned and beloved soldier. Always the
realist, however, Caesar reveals his function in the play when he says
that 'we could not stall together / In the whole world' (39-40) and that
their 'stars' were 'Unreconciliable' (46-7): one had to defeat the
other. Yet Caesar laments 'my brother, my competitor / In top of all
design, my mate in empire, / Friend and companion in the front of
war, / The arm of mine own body, and the heart / Where mine his
thoughts did kindle'. The list goes on too long for comfort as Caesar
tries to give public expression to his private feelings. The whole
sentence (40-8) is fragmented, its grammar disturbed because Caesar
himself is disturbed. The entrance of the messenger from Cleopatra
seems almost a relief to him: he stops his tribute to Antony in
mid-sentence and turns to the 'business' at hand; praise for Antony
can wait for 'some meeter season' (48-51).

Maecenas and Agrippa contribute to the scene's build-up of praise
for Antony (30-3). Decretas, who earlier (IV.xiv.111-13) took Antony's sword to ingratiate himself with Caesar, now appears in a less
callous light. In offering his services to Caesar, he speaks of Antony
as one 'who best was worthy / Best to be served' while he was alive
(6-7). He calls Antony's suicide an act of 'honour' and 'courage' and,
somewhat insolently, offers Caesar the sword 'stained / With his most
noble blood' (20-6). That Caesar apparently does not treat Decretas
as he did the other deserters from Antony shows that he respects him
for such bold talk. Decretas is a practical Roman, but an honest one.

The scene looks ahead to the final scene and must be kept in mind
when judging Cleopatra. Caesar's assurance of 'honourable' and
'kindly' treatment (56-9) is meant mainly for her ears; his own

purpose, as Antony had predicted (IV.xii.33-7), is to capture her alive and lead her in his triumphal procession in Rome. Politically, his plan is astute: the presence of Cleopatra in captivity would detract from any lingering loyalty to Antony and any hostile feelings towards Caesar; Cleopatra, not Caesar, would be seen as the cause of the wars and of Antony's suicide.

At the end of the scene Caesar invites his officers to his tent to examine 'writings' that show how reluctantly ('hardly') he 'was drawn into this war' and how calmly and gently he had dealt with Antony (73-6), but his words must seem hyprocritical when we recall how high-handedly he disposed of Lepidus and broke the treaty with Pompey without informing Antony. 'Honour' or 'reputation' – intrinsic to Antony's being – is for Caesar a matter of public relations; unlike Antony, he is a very modern type of man. At the same time, we wonder why Cleopatra sends her messenger to Caesar. Why has she delayed taking 'the briefest' way (see IV.xv.91) to her death?

Act V, Scene ii

Summary
Cleopatra is still at her monument when Proculeius arrives and tells her to 'fear nothing', for she has 'fall'n into a princely hand'. But, even as they talk, Caesar's soldiers, led by Gallus, enter, seize her, and take the dagger which she has drawn to stab herself. Dolabella arrives to take Proculeius's place, and to him Cleopatra describes her dream of 'an emperor Antony'. So impressed is he by her grief that he tells her Caesar's intention to 'lead' her 'in triumph' in Rome. Caesar and his men now enter, and he promises her and her children 'gentle' treatment if she does not take 'Antony's course'. Cleopatra offers him a list of her treasures; but, when she calls upon her treasurer Seleucus to confirm the list, he demurs. She is angered and shamed by this public betrayal by her own servant, but Caesar tells her that he is not interested in her possessions, which she may keep. After he leaves, Cleopatra tells her attendants that she is well aware that Caesar just 'words' or flatters her – a distrust that proves right when Dolabella informs her that Caesar plans to send her and her children to Rome by way of Syria.

Left alone with her attendants, Charmian and Iras, Cleopatra asks a guard to permit a 'rural fellow' (a 'clown') to enter with a basket of figs; the basket actually contains poisonous asps. Cleopatra calls for her robe and crown; she applies the asps to her breast and arm, but not before Iras falls dead, presumably from grief. Guards rush in and find Charmian rearranging Cleopatra's crown; she too dies, having also applied an asp to herself. The guards call Dolabella, who realizes that what Caesar feared has taken place. Caesar arrives with his train; and, though shorn of the glory of taking Cleopatra alive, he is impressed by the tableau before him. He promises to bury Cleopatra 'by her Antony' in a funeral of 'great solemnity'.

Commentary

The death of Cleopatra is more complicated than that of Antony; it dominates the end of the play. Antony's death restores him to his former greatness, and Cleopatra's increases her in stature. She does nothing that is not true to her character, and yet everything she does raises her to a higher plane. She dies for love and for reunion with Antony ('I am again for Cydnus, / To meet Mark Antony', 228-9), yet to the end she is the same cunning, mysterious Queen whose love of play-acting turns her death into a great piece of theatre.

After Antony died in her arms, there was no doubting her resolve to die: 'Come, we have no friend / But resolution, and the briefest end' (IV.xv.90-1). She now looks forward to 'A better life' than the 'desolation' of this one (1-2); but her 'end', in this the longest scene of the play, is far from brief. Why does she delay? She is aware that she can have no hope of coming to terms with Caesar; bargaining is futile. Gallus's surprise attack, even as Proculeius is trying to beguile her with promises of Caesar's gentleness, and Dolabella's admission that Caesar plans to 'lead' her 'in triumph' in Rome (32-6, 109-10) show that neither she nor her children can expect mercy; she is too shrewd not to see through Caesar: 'He words me, girls, he words me, that I should not / Be noble to myself' (191-2). Before Caesar's arrival, she had asked to 'Look him i' the face' (32). Why? She can hardly hope to influence him.

It is obvious that Cleopatra is playing an elaborate game, and the reason is not far to seek: to outwit Caesar and then take her own life is at once to deny him his final triumph and to pay tribute to Antony. In one respect, the great length of this scene tends to put Antony's death into the background; in another, it justifies his life. For Cleopatra to have taken 'the briefest end', committing suicide immediately out of grief for Antony, would be a movingly impulsive act; but, if her death is to have any meaning for Antony's 'reputation', she must die as the great Queen of Egypt – the beauty who enthralled Julius Caesar, Pompey the Great, and Mark Antony, and who conquered the 'most absurd intents' (226) of Octavius Caesar. This is her way of meeting death 'after the high Roman fashion' (IV.xv.87). She has planned not only the easiest way to die – more 'Egyptian' than 'Roman' – but also one that will not leave her disfigured. After she has confronted Caesar, she will be eager for 'the briefest end'. Once she has the poisonous asps, she is impatient for for the rustic who brought them to leave; as he jabbers on about 'the joy o' the worm', she keeps wishing him 'farewell' (260-80). Once he leaves, she calls for her robe and crown so that death can be proud to take her (281-2). Caesar later is surprised to discover no sign of death upon her ('she looks like sleep', 346). His admiration for an act that 'levelled at our purposes' (336) outweighs his frustration at having lost this most prized of all captives. Her manner of death ennobles her and Antony, too. Caesar orders them to be buried together. Antony and Cleopatra do not merely earn their place 'i' the story', as Enobarbus put it (III.xiii. 46); they *are* the story. Caesar's own story does not seem important at the end; Cleopatra has made an 'ass' (308) of him.

Throughout the scene, then, Cleopatra stages a magnificent show that redounds to the credit of Antony; it was no ordinary person he loved but a 'lass unparalled' (317), Charmian's lovely phrase that captures at once Cleopatra's uniqueness and her common humanity. That is why their deaths do not leave us with that sense of metaphysical terror or incomprehension that we often associate with the endings of tragedy. Although Caesar wins the world, the lovers, by their transcendent deaths, make Caesar's achievements look 'paltry' (2). Shortly before she applies the asps, Cleopatra says, 'I am fire and air – my other elements / I give to baser life' (290-1); her words recall Antony's when he said that he would fight Caesar anywhere – 'i' the fire or i' the air' (IV.x.3-4, and see Commentary). At such moments each reaches insights that lift them above the 'terrene moon' (Antony, III. xiii.153) or 'the fleeting moon' (Cleopatra in this scene, 240), above 'our dungy earth' to a 'new heaven, new earth' (I.i.17, 35). Furthermore, in coming to terms with Antony's 'Romanness', Cleopatra transcends her own 'Egyptianness'; images of Rome and Egypt blend in her dying scene, as in Antony's, to defy simple definitions. Her death is an elaborate ritual 'after the high Roman fashion', but taking the asps to herself is one of the 'easy ways to die' that seem more Egyptian than Roman. (In *Julius Caesar*, Brutus's wife Portia swallowed burning coals.) In the play's symbolism, Rome stands for marriage, Egypt for love; but Antony dies a 'bridegroom' running to his death 'As to a lover's bed' (IV.XIV.100-1), and Cleopatra dies as his bride: 'Husband, I come. / Now to that name, my courage prove my title!' (288-9). At Actium she lost courage and fled; now her courageous act, worthy of a Roman, earns her the right to think of herself as Antony's wife. And, as with Antony's, her death combines the spiritual and the sexual; the clown's bawdy dialogue uses the asp (the 'worm') as a phallic symbol; and Cleopatra, indeed, has 'joy o' the worm' (243-80). Finally, in death, Cleopatra becomes, like 'cold' Octavia, 'marble-constant' (240), her great energy immobilized into the semblance of a statue, but still looking as if, in Caesar's words, 'she would catch another Antony' (347). Before applying the asp herself, Charmian performs the final and most beautiful act of homage: she sets straight her mistress's crown so that Cleopatra looks the queen even in death (319-20; compare, too, 227).

3 THEMES

It is easier to say what *Antony and Cleopatra* is not, rather than what it is, about. We find no clash of good and evil, no metaphysical soul-searching, no vision of terror; instead, the play shows two conflicting modes of life, summed up in the words 'Roman' and 'Egyptian', each with its defenders and detractors. As spectators or as readers, we experience both modes; and the play's meaning derives from the total impact of that experience, which has been carefully guided by the dramatic techniques of structure, characterisation, and language. (In the theatre, the actors also act as our guides.) These techniques force us to take in opposing viewpoints, to consider what there is of value in them, and to suspend easy judgements. The Critical Commentaries on each scene have explored in some detail the connexion between themes and techniques; however, it seems appropriate to bring together, in this section and in the next, the ideas traced earlier so that from the tangle of forty-two scenes we can come to a more focused and comprehensive view of the play. One can approach the matter of themes from other perspectives, such as: the question of greatness, the power of love, and the matter of empire. 'Rome' and 'Egypt' are meant to be only suggestive.

3.1 ROME; EGYPT: ALTERNATIVE CODES OF BEHAVIOUR

Most of *Antony and Cleopatra* takes place in Rome and Alexandria, with brief excursions to Misenum, Parthia, Athens, and Actium. The protagonists operate in a world setting, and the movement from one place to another gives the action epic sweep and grandeur. The love affair between Antony, one of the three rulers of the Roman Empire, and Cleopatra, the Queen of Egypt, can never be private: they are among the world's great people, and their love affects world history just as dynastic rivalry affects their love. Antony's return to Egypt after his marriage to Octavia paves the way for Caesar to declare war on his only significant rival for sole command of the Roman Empire and thereby fulfil what he believes to be his historical destiny. Antony and Cleopatra address one another in terms of their world status: Antony, on his way back to Rome from Egypt, sends an 'orient pearl' to Cleopatra with the message: 'Say the firm Roman to great Egypt sends / This treasure of an oyster' (I.v.43-4).

Rome and Egypt, however, represent more than physical places; they symbolize opposing value systems and codes of behaviour. It would be too narrow a view of the play to say that it is *about* the clash between these systems and codes, but the terms conveniently stand for seemingly endless contrasts and antitheses that confront the characters and explain their actions: public and private; the state and the individual; reason and emotion; mind and heart; intellect and sense; honour and love; duty and pleasure; moderation and excess; reality and imagination; fact and dream; masculine and feminine; war and play; time and timelessness; marriage and love (or sex); Stoicism and Epicureanism; youth and age; striving and rest; death and life. The contrasts appear infinite, and any student of the play will find others.

The words 'Rome' and 'Roman' are associated with the rule of empire and the need for order, law, discipline, and judgement. They are the values that enabled Rome to conquer most of the known world and to inaugurate in the reign of Augustus Caesar (the name given to Octavius after his triumph over Antony) the long period of the *Pax Romana*, the Roman Peace that brought stability to a network of far-flung provinces. To achieve and maintain empire is to be practical, far-sighted, efficient, ruthless if necessary, not romantic or chivalrous. It means knowing oneself, knowing one's enemy, and being prepared to take advantage of the moment. Caesar lives in a world of hard facts and calculations, and he wins. His role requires a denial of private feelings for the public good and for his own success. Caesar succeeds because he does not surrender himself to the emotion of the moment; unlike Antony, the 'child o' the time', he would rather 'possess' time (II.vii.104-5), seize, control, and measure it. The first sentence of the play stresses the high Roman evaluation of 'measure' (I.1.1-2).

If he fails, or chooses not to live by, the Roman standards of measure and self-discipine that win for Caesar the world, Antony nevertheless is devoted to the most notable of all Roman virtues: honour. A good man's name – his reputation – is all; without it, he is nothing. Although his 'full heart' remains with Cleopatra in Egypt, Antony returns to Rome when 'The strong necessity of time commands' his 'services awhile' and his 'honour calls' (I.iii.42-4, 97); the salvation of the Triumvirate depends on his 'absolute soldiership'. 'If I lose mine honour', he tells Octavia, 'I lose myself' (III. iv.22-3). Pompey refuses to believe that Antony would leave Egypt to aid

Caesar and Lepidus in their struggle against him, but for Antony this is an 'honourable trial'. When they meet later, Antony thanks Pompey for recalling him from the 'soft' Eastern beds (II.vi.50-2). To swerve from the call of honour will cause Antony's greatest moment of despair (III. xi.49-50). Throughout the play, Antony never chooses Egypt over Rome although he physically leaves Rome and returns to Egypt; his suicide is not an act of desperation but an heroic act to restore the Roman reputation that he has 'offended': 'a Roman, by a Roman / Valiantly vaquished' are almost his last words (IV.xv. 57-8).

The words 'Egypt' and 'Egyptian', on the other hand, indicate a private, leisurely world where personal feelings have free play, a world of epicurean delights (see II.i.24). Antony's Roman wife, Octavia, 'is of a holy, cold, and still conversation' (II.vi.124-6); but Egyptian scenes show Cleopatra in her 'infinite variety', chiding, laughing, weeping (II.ii.237 and I.i.49-50). Unlike the Roman world of restraint, Egypt is a place where sexual pleasures are openly acknowledged. There is also a mythic timeless quality about Shakespeare's Egypt, where soothsayers and prophecies and dreams count for more than hard facts. Here Cleopatra daydreams of Antony when he is away (I.v.19-27), and here she dreams of 'an emperor Antony' when he is dead (V.ii.76-92). Not just 'scarce-bearded Caesar' but Rome itself is young – active, ambitious, striving, creating history – compared to the older civilization of Egypt, whose pyramids stand eternal ('wrinkled deep in time' like Cleopatra herself, I.v.29), unaffected by time, as other nations rise and fall at Fortune's will (see Cleopatra's comment on Caesar's being 'Fortune's knave', V.ii.2-4). Egypt, like Cleopatra, appeals to the imagination: the Romans are fascinated by it; and Enobarbus, the man of reason, is carried away in describing its Queen in the most famous passage in the play (II.ii.191-241). In this paradoxical land, the Nile 'o'erflows', breeding poisonous serpents but also promising rich harvests from its slimy banks (II.vii.22-5). Here Antony's 'pleasure lies' (II.iii.41), and here his heart comes to rest.

3.2 ROME OR EGYPT: THE NATURE OF JUDGEMENT

'Rome' and 'Egypt' in *Antony and Cleopatra* symbolize the extreme definitions by which human beings can take stock of their lives – 'Rome' of the outer being, 'Egypt' of the inner. Taken together, they sum up the possibilities for human fulfilment. But precisely because they symbolize extreme responses, they cannot adequately represent the complexities and realities of everyday human behaviour. Is any human being completely 'Roman' or

'Egyptian'? If anyone is, he or she seems unfinished, even comic. Caesar, the archetypal Roman of the play, is essentially a comic character. His unbending allegiance to the Roman code simplifies his life by justifying his single-minded ambition and by providing him with a publicly acknowledged set of moral judgements that he can cite as he rides roughshod over Pompey, Lepidus, Antony, Cleopatra – over anyone who stands in the way of his final triumph. Cleopatra, the archetypal Egyptian, is more complex because the 'inner' being is always something of a mystery compared to the 'outer', but she provides the highest comedy of the play. It is only when she comes to appreciate fully what 'Rome' means to Antony that, without denying whatever is 'Egyptian' about her, she becomes worthy of sharing the title of the play with him. The magnificent last scene in which she outwits Caesar is, as much a tribute to Antony's 'Roman-ness' as to her own 'Egyptian-ness'; in it she becomes a genuine tragic heroine.

Antony straddles both worlds, Rome and Egypt; and, with the lesser exception of Enobarbus, whose own plight highlights Antony's, he is, until Cleopatra joins him in her 'resolution' to commit suicide, the only truly tragic character in the play because of the claims that both worlds, embodied in Caesar and in Cleopatra, have upon him. To choose either Rome or Egypt makes him a lesser human being. The first scene of the play makes it clear that Cleopatra is an ordering principle of his life, but the second scene makes it clear that Rome is also. At his death, *in Cleopatra's arms*, the same still holds true; his suicide is a noble *Roman* act. In the third scene, when he finally makes the 'break' with Cleopatra (a 'break' which, as Enobarbus recognizes, he will not be able to endure), he tells her that he goes 'from hence, / Thy soldier, servant, making peace or war / As thou affects' (I.iii.69-71). Cleopatra's love ennobles him and at the same time makes his activity as a Roman soldier meaningful. Balancing, however fragilely, Egyptian love and Roman honour, Antony is at such moments a complete man – the only one in the play. Later, significantly, he wins his one military victory against Caesar after Cleopatra arms him (IV.iv., vii, and viii). Without Rome, Antony is incomplete, but without Cleopatra – as Enobarbus tells us time and again – he is also incomplete. Enobarbus chooses Rome, the side of reason, and dies broken-hearted. It would be wrong to say, however, that Antony's return to Cleopatra is the choice of Egypt over Rome: both worlds will separately disappoint him, but he will die in harmony with both.

Antony's mingling of Roman and Egyptian ideals at their best makes a mockery of the terms when they are worshipped separately. Cleopatra herself praises Antony's 'heavenly mingle' (I.v.59). Throughout the play, however, the Romans judge the Egyptians, the Egyptians the Romans – almost always from a negative, exclusionary point of view, since to regard others in terms of labels is to reduce their humanity: both judges and judged become victims of language. The Romans are the worst offenders. Rulers of the world, made smug by conquest, and exalting mind over heart, they are the great moralizers of the play; but Antony's 'heavenly mingle' and Cleopatra's 'infinite variety' raise them above formulas and make most moral judgements of them seem inadequate. Antony and Cleopatra turn out to be, in a sense, more 'moral' than those who pass moral judgements on them: magnanimity, compassion, and selfessness are evidence of a deeper morality than Caesar is capable of.

Because of the stature that Antony and Cleopatra attain by their deaths, some critics consider the play more of a tragi-comedy or even a 'divine comedy' than a genuine tragedy. Nevertheless, a tragedy it is, however glowing the ending: only in death can the two lovers fulfil the vision they have of themselves, and the life of either without the other would be a kind of death-in-life. Cleopatra learns too late what 'Roman' signifies: without his 'Roman-ness', Antony would not have been the man she loved. Antony does not have to learn the significance of 'Roman' or 'Egyptian', but he is unable to devote himself to being one or the other with the kind of single-mindedness that drives Caesar to the successful attainment of his ambition; that is Antony's tragedy – but also his glory. Only in death can he be the complete person that he sought to be in life, where both worlds, Rome and Egypt, have been something of a disappointment to him. In Antony's 'new heaven, new earth', 'Where souls do couch on flowers', even Aeneas, who chose honour over love, will be reunited to Dido, contrary to their story in Virgil's *Aeneid* (IV.xiv.51-4; see also I.i.17). But in the Roman world of political intrigue, deceit, and betrayal, Antony's devotion to the combined ideal of honour and love seems quixotic. Caesar makes sure that his publicity portrays him as 'honourable' (see V.i.58); but he betrays Lepidus, Pompey, Antony, and, if we believe that he used his own sister as a pawn against Antony, even Octavia. Cleopatra outwits him before he can betray her also. Roman ideals as embodied in actual human beings do not approximate to Antony's vision of what it means to be 'Roman'. His defeat in a world contested for by Caesars and Pompeys seems inevitable.

Yet the everyday Egyptian world is inadequate too in its irresponsibility and frivolousness. Cleopatra often refuses to face the truth – amusingly so in her interviews with the messenger who brings her the news of Antony's marriage to Octavia (II.v. and III.iii) and with dire results when she pays no heed to Enobarbus's solid arguments against her participation in the battle at Actium (III.vii. 1-19). When he returns to Egypt, Antony loses his 'absolute soldiership' (III.vii.42); his 'honour' now seems mere recklessness. But, in the end, Antony renounces neither honour nor love, and Caesar comes to look 'paltry' (V.ii.2) in comparison. Antony himself falls short of his ideals; but in choosing to live and die by seemingly incompatible values, he lives heroically and dies tragically.

3.3 BEYOND ROME, BEYOND EGYPT: DEATH AND TRANSFIGURATION

By Roman standards, Antony's suicide is an heroic act, a triumph over himself. Cleopatra understands that this is as 'it should be' (IV.xv.14-17); and, in the play's last scene, she describes her dream of 'an emperor Antony', whose 'face was as the heavens, and therein stuck / A sun and moon, which kept their course and lighted / The little O, the earth'. When she pauses to ask Dolabella whether he thinks that 'there was, or might be such a man / As this I dreamt of', this most compassionate of Caesar's emissaries, himself falling in love with Cleopatra whom he has come to guard, gives the Roman response: 'Gentle madam, no' (V.ii.74-94). Dreams are Egyptian; facts are Roman.

But who is right? Despite his all-too-human flaws, Antony has a generosity of spirit and a zest for living that seem to light up this 'little O, the earth', darkened by Caesar's lack of generosity, his machiavellian politics, and his obsessive, single-minded ambition. Lest we become sentimental, however, we should recognize that the Antony we see on the stage – no matter how imposing the actor playing the part might be – is hardly the godlike creature of Cleopatra's dream. Antony's devotion to the Roman ideal of honour is noble, but his living by that ideal makes him seem for much of the play absurd or irrational. Nothing reveals his earthbound humanity more than the sight of Cleopatra and her attendants drawing up his mortally-doomed body to the top of her monument. 'How heavy weighs my lord!', says Cleopatra; and the guards express what the audience must feel: 'A heavy sight!' (IV.xv.30-40). Much in the play supports Dolabella's 'Gentle madam, no'. The stage Antony is no colossus whose 'legs bestrid the ocean', whose 'reared arm / Crested the world' (V.ii.82-3), but at times a weary, middle-aged man who feels that time is running out for him and desperately wants 'one other gaudy night' (III.xiii.183). Cleopatra, for whose love Antony has put his 'honour' at stake, often appears petty, selfish, and absurd – not the goddess whom Enobarbus describes as beggaring 'all description' and 'O'erpicturing' (excelling) any portrait that an artist could imagine of Venus (II.ii.198-202). Only *after* Antony's death does she become truly splendid in her resolve to die 'after the high Roman fashion'.

Both 'Roman' and 'Egyptian' judgements are supported by enough evidence in the play to make each seem right, or wrong, or insufficient. Even the exemplar of Roman judgement, Caesar himself, is guilty of misjudgements: he misjudges Cleopatra and is cheated of his final triumph. Enobarbus chooses the side of reason, and dies broken-hearted. Fulvia's death makes Antony realize that 'There's a great spirit gone!' (I.ii.123). In an ever-changing world, judgements seem unreliable. But where does this leave the audience or the reader? What are we, finally, to make of Antony and Cleopatra? In the medieval morality plays, which Shakespeare must have known, a character like the doctor at the end of *Everyman* would tell the audience what the play was about. Shakespeare presents the complexities of life and leaves us to infer meanings; but he does provide guideposts, and one appears in Cleopatra's rebuke to Dolabella (who has denied her word-portrait of Antony):

> You lie, up to the hearing of the gods.
> But if there be or ever were one such,
> It's past the size of dreaming. Nature wants stuff
> To vie strange forms with fancy, yet to imagine
> An Antony were nature's piece 'gainst fancy,
> Condemning shadows quite.   (V.ii.95-100)

What Cleopatra seems to be saying in this difficult passage is that the human mind can outdo nature in fancying – or imagining or dreaming – 'strange forms' that nowhere exist; but the Antony of whom she dreams is nature's greatest triumph over mere human fancying; he is greater even than her dream. In other words, the Antony of her dream is closer to the true Antony than the one Dolabella knows: Dolabella's Antony, the one we are familiar with, is but a shadow of the truth. The Antony we see and hear in the play is the *actual* Antony, but the *real* Antony is the one closer to Cleopatra's dream. Yet nature always works with what is actual: it 'wants stuff / To vie strange forms with fancy'. Nature creates from what is already there, and the actual Antony already kindles the imagination of everyone with whom he comes into contact, not just Cleopatra but all the Romans, too. Antony is 'that great med'cine' whose 'tinct' gilds everyone (I.v.35-7). The actual Antony is a man with the potential of his ancestral god Hercules (see IV.iii) but never realizing that potential 'Beneath the visiting moon' (IV.xv.68).

   Cleopatra's 'dream' is an act of love, which also invites us to dream, and love, with her, to go beyond facile moralizing and to participate in Antony's and her own magnanimity. The *real* Antony and the *real* Cleopatra are not the poor figures (even the best of actors) on the bare stage of the Globe theatre but the Antony and Cleopatra in our minds. In one of Shakespeare's boldest strokes, Cleopatra takes us right to the Globe theatre when she gives her reasons for never letting Caesar take her back to Rome where

> Antony
> Shall be brought drunken forth, and I shall see
> Some squeaking Cleopatra boy my greatness
> I' the posture of a whore   (V.ii.218-21)

Today's audience, watching an attractive actress in the role of Cleopatra, finds it hard to imagine that the Cleopatra on Shakespeare's stage was a twelve- to fourteen-year-old boy actor (though one whose voice presumably had not yet begun to squeak!). To picture Cleopatra as only a boy actor breaks the spell and momentarily deflates her role, but it shows us how inadequate is the 'actual': the imaginary Cleopatra beggars 'all description' (II.ii.199), and like the imaginary Antony she is more real than the actual. To glimpse the real in the actual is the work of the imagination to which the play pays tribute.

4 DRAMATIC TECHNIQUES

4.1 STRUCTURE AND STAGECRAFT

Our word 'theatre' derives from the Greek word that means to 'see'; and in a theatre audiences literally *see* the meaning of the play, as its plot, brought to life on the stage, unfolds before their eyes. The division of *Antony and Cleopatra* into five separate acts and forty-two scenes is the work of modern editors; this conventional division, however, obscures the real structure of the play. As originally published in the First Folio of 1623, it had no divisions at all; and this is how it was staged at the Globe theatre. Shakespeare's audience saw, in effect, a one-act play, probably performed with no intervals and moving swiftly on an open, uncurtained stage with no scenery. (see *Appendix: Shakespeare's theatre*). The action alternated between Rome and Egypt, with brief excursions elsewhere, and the scenes flowed one into the other, without any noticeable pauses between them – like a motion picture today. The Critical Commentary above points out in detail the relevance of this flow and juxtaposition of scenes to the play's meaning.

We cannot be absolutely sure that the play originally was performed in this manner although substantial evidence exists for this view; but let us imagine that, as a group of characters from one scene in Egypt exits through one of the doors at the back of the stage, another group in Rome enters simultaneously from another door. It would thus be possible for spectators to *see* Rome and Egypt together in the same space at the same time. (If the stage were actually empty between scenes, as some scholars believe, the pause would still likely be minimal.) Consider, then, the effect at the end of what we now call Act I, scene iii, as Antony, in Egypt, is taking leave from Cleopatra to depart for Rome. His last words, as they leave the stage, are:

> Let us go. Come.
> Our separation so abides and flies
> That thou, residing here, goes yet with me;
> And I, hence fleeting, here remain with thee.
> Away!

The stage direction for the next scene (I.iv) is:
Enter OCTAVIUS CAESAR, *reading a letter,* LEPIDUS, *and their train.*

For a fleeting moment, perhaps, Antony and Cleopatra in Egypt occupy the same stage with Caesar and Lepidus in Rome. Caesar's first words are about Antony, his 'great competitor'. Caesar wants him back in Rome as much as Cleopatra wants to keep him with her in Egypt. The juxtaposition of these two scenes shows that Rome's claim on Antony is as compelling as Egypt's: wherever he resides, Antony carries Rome and Egypt with him. In a motion picture, the effect would be that of one scene fading out as the next phase of the action is momentarily transposed upon it and then takes over. But whereas in a motion picture your eyes may be riveted upon spectacular settings, the pyramids of Egypt or the Roman Forum, Shakespeare's stage remains neutrally bare in both scenes. There may not even be a noticeable difference in costume. No one knows what the eunuchs fanning Cleopatra in the first scene looked like; there was just a stab at historical or regional costuming. For the most part, actors wore contemporary Elizabethan or Jacobean garb, suitable to the rank and social class of the wearer, no matter where or when the action took place. Cleopatra orders Charmian to 'Cut my lace' (I.iii.71); and Antony angrily asks Cleopatra, after what he thinks is her excessive display of courtesy to Thidias, 'To flatter Caesar, would you mingle eyes / With one that ties his points?' (or laces for fastening clothes, III.xiii.156-7) – references to Jacobean rather than to Egyptian or Roman dress.

On the Globe stage Rome and Egypt were not so much *places* as *states of mind* . The shifting back and forth of scenes forces upon us multiple perspectives so that we cannot accept one viewpoint as definitive. Shakespeare's epic stage becomes the focus of an epic of the psyche, the stage of the world reduced to the mind of man, with Antony at the centre of an interior battle. The public world of Rome and the private world of Egypt co-exist in his mind and heart. It is not that Antony chooses Egypt in I.i and then turns around and chooses Rome in I.ii: he makes no choice at all, nor can he bring the two together successfully for very long. His tragedy is that others constantly force him to make a choice that denies him his completeness as a human being. He resists, and the world defeats him. Most of Act II shows Antony absorbed in the Roman world; he even marries into it. This act has only one Egyptian scene, II.v; it shows Cleopatra shortly after Antony's betrothal to Octavia and just before the unified Triumvirate meets Pompey, and it casts an ironic perspective on the other scenes. The next time we see Cleopatra is in III.iii, which turns out to be a continuation of II.v. The link between these two scenes brings home the point that while Antony is busy in Rome Cleopatra is working to win him back. Midway through the play, somewhere between III.iv and III.vii, Antony breaks with Rome and returns to Egypt (see the Critical Commentary for details). From here on, the action moves swiftly to Antony's defeat and suicide, with a large number of very short scenes alternating between Caesar's and Antony's camps. 'The miserable change now at my end' that Antony refers to as he lies dying in Cleopatra's arms (IV.xv.51) comes about rapidly as Caesar wrests time away from Antony, the 'child o' the time' (II.vii.104). In his final scenes (IV.xiv and xv), a remarkable calm comes over Antony as he transcends, in death, the struggle to harmonize Rome and Egypt.

Although Cleopatra shares the play's title with him, until the end of the fourth act Antony alone is the tragic hero. But then Shakespeare does something totally unexpected: he gives almost the whole fifth act, the very long second scene, over to Cleopatra. The leisurely pace of this final scene, the longest in the play, brings a sense of rest and transcendence after the hectic rush of scenes through the third and fourth acts. Here Cleopatra fully enters the realm of tragedy and deservedly earns her place in the title. To the end she retains her 'infinite variety', still providing high comedy as she outwits Caesar but ultimately revealing the magnificence that so often in the play we had to take on faith. She dies the great lover and the majestic Queen of Egypt. Even Caesar is impressed. This last scene completely reverses Philo's and Demetrius's Roman judgement of her, in the first scene, as a lustful 'gypsy'. She vindicates Antony's faith in her, and now she joins him in the 'new heaven, new earth' beyond 'our dungy earth' (I.i.17,35) that could not contain their love or their greatness.

4.2 CHARACTERISATION

In Shakespeare's primary source for the play, *The Life of Marcus Antonius*, the Greek biographer Plutarch (c.46 – 120 A.D.) shows us the attractive sides of Antony and Cleopatra; but he leaves no doubt that Antony, because of his 'unreined lust' and 'vain love' for Cleopatra, deserved to lose his share of the empire to Caesar and that Cleopatra committed suicide not to honour Antony but only after she realized that she could not influence Caesar. Shakespeare's complex method of characterisation, on the other hand, even while it shows us the defects of the two lovers, ultimately renders all summary judgements and moralisations unsatisfactory: the play acknowledges their frailties as human beings, but the scope of their passions and their zest for living render them more attractively human than any other character. Paradoxically, their very humanity makes them seem larger than life in a world where they are surrounded by characters of less 'infinite variety' (II.ii.237); even the almighty Caesar, their conqueror and the world's, shrinks in comparison. Shakespeare shows us that both Antony and Cleopatra have an enormous capacity for feeling that makes them vulnerable and ripe for tragedy; at the same time his selection of details reveals the warm humanity that compels love, admiration, and loyalty and that invests their personal tragedies with dignity. Both are great stage presences, who enliven their scenes with vigorous displays of deeply-felt emotions. Enobarbus dies broken-hearted because he has rejected the heart for reason; Antony and Cleopatra die redeemed by the largeness not only of their love but also of their visions of a fully engaged and complete life. Roman judgement of them, Antony in particular, often smacks of envy.

The structure of the play (see above), with its constantly shifting perspectives, affects the characterisation. The way that scenes follow one another, often contradicting what has gone before or putting things in a new light, keeps us from seeing or interpreting or judging from any single point of view, Roman or Egyptian, any character. All the major characters invite contradictory responses, none more so than Antony and Cleopatra. The secondary characters are more simply, though often vividly, sketched since their primary function is to illuminate or to give context to the actions of the major characters (see the Critical Commentaries for Pompey, II.i, vi, vii; Octavia, II.iii, III.ii, iv; Lepidus, I.iv, II.ii, vii, III.ii, vi; Charmian and Iras, I.ii, iii, V.ii; Eros, IV.xiv; Thidias, III.xiii; Ventidius, III.i; Dolabella, V.ii; Philo, I.i; Soothsayer, I.ii, II.iii; Clown, V.ii).

Caesar

Caesar is neither villain nor hero. Shortly before engaging Antony in battle he says, 'The time of universal peace is near' (IV.vi.5), and in Shakespeare's day Renaissance humanists knew Augustus Caesar as the emperor who established the *Pax Romana*, a long period of peace and cultural achievement. James I, who came to the English throne in 1603, liked to think of himself as the 'new Augustus'; he re-named Shakespeare's company, the Lord Chamberlain's Men, the King's Men. Is Shakespeare's portrayal of Caesar an ironic comment on the new king? Cleopatra says, ' 'Tis paltry to be Caesar' (V.ii.2), and Antony scorns him for having 'kept / His sword e'en like a dancer' at Philippi, and for relying on his 'lieutenantry' to do the fighting rather than himself engaging 'in the brave squares of war' (III.xi, 35-40). Antony is both right and wrong; Caesar is not the 'absolute' soldier that Antony is, but he is the better strategist, politically and militarily, and it is his capable use of his officers that wins him an empire. Unbending and obsessive in his pursuit of power, he appears in the play as 'paltry', almost a comic figure, because we have no sense of his inner life, his completeness as a human being.

Enobarbus

Enobarbus is often cited as 'the voice of reason' in the play; when Antony's 'valour preys on reason', he decides to desert him (III.xiii, 199-201). Yet Enobarbus dies ingloriously in 'Some ditch' (IV.vi.38), twice calling Antony's name as his last words (IV.ix.23). Like Caesar, Enobarbus lives for the public life, although he admits that the spoils of war are what interest him, as when he greets the 'famous pirate' Menas: 'But give me your hand, Menas. If our eyes had authority [to arrest us], here they might take two thieves kissing' (II.vi.95-7). Unlike Caesar, however, he has an inner life which he refuses to acknowledge until it is too late. Despite himself, from time to time his private passions surface. Early in the play, he mocks what he believes is Antony's facile ability to weep at will (III.ii.57-9); but later, when Antony is thanking his 'household servants' for their loyalty, Enobarbus himself cannot refrain from weeping although he tries to make light of it by blaming Antony for creating such a sentimental moment (IV.ii.33-6). Weeping threatens his Roman masculinity. Although he calls Cleopatra Antony's 'Egyptian dish' (II.vi.128), it may not be a surprise that the play's most glorious evocation of Cleopatra, as the goddess of love, comes from Enobarbus, who clearly reveals that he, like Antony, has fallen under her spell (II.ii.191-241). He has good 'reasons' to desert Antony, but he soon learns that the heart has its own more compelling reasons. After his betrayal, nothing is left for him but, in his own words, to 'Think, and die' (III.xiii.1).

Cleopatra

If Caesar has no private passions, and Enobarbus is unwilling to admit or to give play to his, Cleopatra is almost all private passion. Of all the characters in the play, she is the most mysterious (as befits someone who lives for private satisfactions) and the most para-doxical. Agrippa reacts to Enobarbus's wonderful description of her first meeting with Antony 'upon the river of Cydnus' with an admiring phrase that contains the essence of her contradictions: 'Royal wench!' (II.ii.227). Like all the Romans, who automatically denigrate Cleopatra, he is fascinated by her, even at second-hand, and, it seems, is somewhat envious of Antony. At her death, dressed regally in her robe and crown, Cleopatra appears to Charmian 'A lass unparalleled' (V.ii.317) – another such phrase that captures her common humanity and her uniqueness. After Antony dies in her arms, she wants to be thought of as 'No more but e'en a woman, and commanded / By such poor passion as the maid that milks / And does the meanest chares' (IV.xv.73–5); she dies, however, as befits a Queen of Egypt, in a splendid spectacle that dazzles even Caesar. To the end, Antony never completely understands her, and she recognizes that: although we can empathise with his rage when he sees her offering her hand to Thidias, she asks him, 'Not know me yet?' (III.xiii.157). Except for momentary flare-ups of jealousy and anger, Antony, to his credit, simply accepts her for the person she is – and that, after all, is what love is all about.

Yet, until her final scene, although nothing in her behaviour warrants the Roman view of her as a lustful 'gypsy' (I.i.9), the character whom we see on the stage hardly justifies Antony's infatuation. Enobarbus's goddess is a vision, not the stage reality. For most of the play, Cleopatra fails to comphrend the imperative of 'honour' that summons Antony back to Rome or what the word 'Roman' means to his conception of himself. Defying Enobarbus's advice, she insists on participating as Antony's equal at Actium with results that are disastrous (III.x). When Antony is in deepest despair, she publicly shows favour to Caesar's ambassador, who has come asking for Antony's head (III.xiii); and, although she promises to make 'the briefest end' for herself after Antony's suicide (IV.xv.91), for a long while, in the final scene, she gives the impression of negotiating with Caesar for favourable terms.

At the same time, Cleopatra elicits our sympathy as a mature woman of the world who knows how vulnerable love makes its victims: she had seen Julius Caesar and Pompey the Great leave her and go back to Rome, never to return, and in Antony's behaviour towards Fulvia and Octavia she sees what possibly lies in store for her. From the beginning, her deep and abiding love for Antony comes across as genuine: he is an obsession with her, as she is for him, and the time that he is away hangs heavy on her hands (see I.v. and II.v). After Actium, for most of Act III until the final scene of Act IV, she seems to shrink from Antony's anger and almost fades away. But the whole point of her characterisation is this: that the more difficult she is to fathom, the more faith is required to love and believe in her. Antony does not look for 'reasons' to love Cleopatra; he just does. Loving her is not the 'business' that he and Caesar understand his marriage to Octavia to be (see II.ii.167). Antony's faith, though Cleopatra sorely tests it at times, never really wavers: he asks for no explanations from her and sees no need ever to 'pardon' her (see III.xi.68-70). At the end, her triumph over Caesar and her supreme sacrifice justify his faith.

Antony

Precisely because neither public nor private passions exclusively define him, Antony sometime appears to be an inconsistent character. In the first scene of the play he seems to have succumbed entirely to Egypt and love; in the second he unhesitatingly answers the call of Rome and 'honour'. But Antony is not inconsistent; he simply refuses stereotyping. Neither Rome nor Egypt adequately defines him. Unlike Caesar, he is not driven or consumed by public passions; unlike Cleopatra, he is not limited or narrowed by private ones. And, unlike Enobarbus, he not only acknowledges the demands of his inner self, but his personal code of generosity, loyalty, courtesy, and gratitude also informs his public role, just as his public role gives meaning to his inner being: without a good name – 'reputation' (see III.xi.49, and Critical Commentary) – he is nothing. Antony has no conflict with himself; what he finds incomprehensible is Cleopatra's erratic behaviour and Caesar's mockery of Roman ideals in his betrayal of oaths and total pursuit of power by any means. It is not going too far to say that Antony is the only completely realized human being in the play – that is, until Cleopatra finally comes to realize that his greatness is not the exclusive property of Rome or Egypt and decides to follow him in death 'after the high Roman fashion'. Her last scene is her tribute to Antony. She has learned from him how to be complete herself.

Antony as a tragic hero poses a problem for criticism. Typically, the hero of tragedy is engaged in a search for meaning that ultimately brings about a new awareness of the world and of the self. The unquestioning hero belongs more properly to the world of comedy. Antony, however, is not the tortured soul who (like Hamlet, for instance) feels divided between his public and private selves: he feels comfortable as both soldier *and* lover, but his tragedy turns out to be that the world will not let him live in the genial atmosphere of comedy where he belongs. The world as it exists in the play is too narrow, too self-limiting to contain him; both Rome and Egypt want to lower him to their levels, and he resists. Only a 'new heaven, new earth' – a world beyond this one – offers him the possibility of harmony. The play makes much of the difference in age between Caesar and Antony: some twenty years older, Antony comes across as a man who knows the world and has experienced the whims of fortune. He is not out to conquer the world, and he does not question the gods (as most tragic heroes do). He knows full well that responsibilities are to be fulfilled and that pleasures are to be enjoyed. His is the voice of maturity. He rightly asks, 'My being in Egypt, Caesar, / What was't to you?' (II.ii.35-6).

Several times the Critical Commentary has compared Antony to the medieval knight who fulfils himself as a warrior in the service of a lady whom he worships. Antony himself tells Cleopatra that he is her 'soldier, servant, making peace or war / As thou affects' (I.iii.70-1). As the sixteenth century turned into the seventeenth, what nostalgically was conceived of as England's heroic past was still within reach of memory although that memory was receding. Antony evokes that heroic past. Caesar, in contrast, is an example of the 'new man' of the Renaissance, a figure appearing with increasing frequency in the plays of Shakespeare and his fellow dramatists as the dying feudal system, with its code of personal loyalties and chivalric honour, was being supplanted by the dawning of capitalism, which placed individual success above such loyalties and sworn oaths (Caesar breaks his oath to Lepidus and to Pompey, thus betraying Antony, too). Antony belongs to a more heroic past that included Julius Caesar and Pompey the Great, not lesser characters like Octavius Caesar and Sextus Pompeius.

4.3 LANGUAGE, VERSE, AND IMAGERY

The triumph of Antony and Cleopatra over *both* 'Rome' and 'Egypt' is also the triumph of poetry itself. In death they fulfil their visions of themselves and transcend the prosaic values of this 'dungy earth' which 'alike / Feeds beast as man' (I.i.35-6). The final image of the two lovers is far removed from the play's opening image of them as 'the bellows and the fan / To cool a gypsy's lust' (I.i.9-10). Their 'story' – the one in which Enobarbus had hoped to earn 'a place' (III.xiii.46) – is made complete by their deaths and now resembles a finished work of art, with a beginning, a middle, and an end. As we look back over the whole 'story', we see that Antony and Cleopatra, like the lovers of the 'The Canonization', John Donne's famous poem, offer the world that has never understood them 'A pattern of [their] love'. By a wonderful irony, this pattern turns all judgements around: other characters who had measured them now take their 'measure' (a Roman word; see below) from them. The powerful fall short, and the humble are exalted as even lowly attendants like Eros, Charmian, and Iras earn 'A nobleness in record' (IV.xiv.99).

Yet what is it that compels the admiration for the lovers? The answer in large measure lies in the glory of the language used by others in describing them or by the lovers themselves as they voice their visions of one another. When Dolabella confronts Cleopatra with the implausibility of her dream of 'an emperor Antony' ('Gentle madam, no'), her response that he is lying, 'up to the hearing of the gods' (V.ii.95), has the ring of truth; for her dream – a great poetic evocation of Antony – makes 'defect perfection', as Enobarbus once said of her (II.ii.232). The poetry in passages like these can take us beyond the physical stage and merely human actors and force us to respond not just with our eyes but, even more so, with our hearts and imaginations. Since poetry is the most imaginative way that we can use language, to respond fully and completely to the poetry of Cleopatra's dream means that we, like her, help make 'defect perfection'. At the very least, the poetry of her dream convinces Dolabella of the sincerity of her grief, and he vows to help her.

Frail human beings though they are, Antony and Cleopatra compel admiration for the loftiness of their aspirations – a loftiness matched by a poetry of epic grandeur that complements the epic spaciousness against which their tragedies unfold. Only a 'new heaven, new earth', as Antony says (I.i.17), could contain their love. The play is written in a mixture of poetry and prose. The latter, as is customary in Shakespeare's plays, is used for the more comic and relaxed passages – for the light sexual banter among Cleopatra's attendants (I.ii.1-78, for instance); for the cynical commentaries that Enobarbus and other Roman soldiers make on 'the great fellows' who rule the world (II.ii.172-90 and II.vi.83-139); or for the 'clown' who brings Cleopatra her poisonous asps and taxes her patience (V.ii.245-80). When Antony demands that Enobarbus be serious ('No more light answers') and listen to his reasons for breaking with Cleopatra, prose switches to poetry (I.ii.132-99). Enobarbus's change from prose to poetry when he describes the first meeting of Antony and Cleopatra 'upon the river of Cydnus' (II.ii.187 and following) tells us much about the speaker: like Antony, he is smitten with Cleopatra.

Most of the play, however, is written in Shakespeare's characteristic blank verse – unrhymed lines of ten syllables each, with the accent normally on every second syllable. Most of the characters, Roman and Egyptian, speak in this verse; but, though the formal structure of it (the metre) remains fairly constant, images and rhythms distinguish Romans from Egyptians, and Antony and Cleopatra from everyone else. Their speeches tend to be more expansive, more fluent, grander: they reach for the stars, an image associated with both of them (IV.xiv.106 and V.ii.309).

In general, the images associated with Rome have to do with measure, rule, control, moderation, and containment, while those with Egypt with dissolving, melting, overflowing, and excess. The first line and a half of the play may stand for a summary of this opposition:

> Nay, but this dotage of our general's
> O'erflows the measure.

'Nay' is the first powerful word of the play: the Roman condemnation of Egyptian excess. To Philo, Antony in Egypt has violated the rules of civilized behaviour. When Antony, about to embrace Cleopatra, says, 'Let Rome in Tiber melt, and the wide arch / Of the ranged empire fall! Here is my space. / Kingdoms are clay' (I.i.33-5), to the Romans he appears like a madman. Later, after he becomes engaged to Octavia, Antony returns also to his Romanness; he tells her: 'My Octavia, / Read not my blemishes in the world's report. / I have not kept my square, but that to come / Shall all be done by the rule' (II.iii.4-7). With Cleopatra, he does all from the heart.

To overflow the measure is for the Egyptians to be closer to the creative sources of life – to be fertile, to grow, and to reap harvests. Caesar is disgusted to learn that Cleopatra dresses 'In the habiliments [robes] of the goddess Isis' (III.vi.17), but it suits Cleopatra to appear in public as the Egyptian goddess of the moon (regulating the tides and associated with the menstrual cycle) and of fertility. Ironically, the Egyptians do *measure* 'the flow o'the Nile', as Antony explains to his fellow Romans at Pompey's banquet, but they hope to find that the river will swell and overflow and thereby make the land fertile (II.vii.19-25). The Egyptians are allied by their images to nature, the Romans to civilization; and these alliances tend to affect the way that they talk. Cleopatra, for instance, fondly uses a food image when she boasts of being 'A morsel for a monarch' (I.v.31), but the Romans associate food with sex in a disgusting way, as when Enobarbus tells Menas that 'Antony will to his Egyptian dish again' (II.vi.128); Cleopatra's 'clown' knows 'that a woman is a dish for the gods' (V.ii.275). In his deepest anguish and shame, after Actium, Antony reverts to pure 'Roman': he tells Cleopatra, 'I found you as a morsel, cold upon / Dead Caesar's trencher' (III.xiii.116-17). Sex is as natural as eating to the Egyptians; they talk unshamedly about it. Romans seem fearful about it and disguise their feelings; it represents to them a melting away or dissolving of the self. Love is an even greater threat since no one is more vulnerable than a lover, whose well-being, even identity, comes from being loved – as Antony and Cleopatra know only too well. Romans find Egyptians threatening; Egyptians find Romans stultifying.

To exaggerate either the natural or the civilized involves a cost to the self. Civilization means the controlling of nature and the establishment of rules; but it should not mean the denial of nature, especially human nature. On the other hand, impulsive gratification is destructive of self and civilization. To satisfy self, Cleopatra would 'Melt Egypt into Nile' and turn 'kindly creatures...all to serpents!' (II.v.78-9) just as Antony would 'Let Rome in Tiber melt', each forgetting the many lives for which they are responsible. Antony's temporary loss of both the love and the honour to which he has impulsively given himself results, for a while, in his loss of any identity: he compares himself to the changing clouds which 'cannot hold this visible shape' (IV.xiv.1-14). Before she dies, Cleopatra refers to 'this knot intrinsicate / Of life' which she is about to 'untie' (V.ii.305-6). The unusual word 'intrinsicate' combines two words

– 'intrinsic' and 'intricate'. The play suggests throughout that both Rome and Egypt are *intrinsic* to the complete and harmonious life, but that keeping them in balance is a very *intricate* affair. It is easier to be all Roman or all Egyptian. Caesar hides his tears, and no one knows how he feels; but his driving ambition makes Cleopatra's assessment of him seem plausible: 'Not being Fortune, he's but Fortune's knave, / A minister of her will' (V.ii.3-4). Antony and Cleopatra defy Fortune (see, for instance, III.xi.73-4). Ultimately, as the example of Enobarbus proves, the inner life cannot be denied. On the other hand, Cleopatra comes to understand that Antony's Roman concern for 'honour' or 'reputation' is intrinisic to his greatness, and that for both of them their public and private selves are intricately woven together. Antony has always known that. The tragedy for both of them is that, except for a few brief moments in life, only in death do they achieve the perfection of themselves. Antony dies 'a Roman' but in his Egypt's arms. Cleopatra dies to evocations of marriage and motherhood (V.ii.288, 310-11), but still remaining in her robe and crown the Queen of Egypt.

The tragedies of Antony and Cleopatra also bespeak their greatness. Images associate both of them with light and day: when Antony dies, 'the torch is out' (IV.xiv.46), and 'the bright day is done' when Cleopatra commits suicide (V.ii.193-4). Cleopatra cries out when she sees the dying Antony '*borne by the* GUARD':

> O sun,
> Burn the great sphere thou mov'st in; darkling stand
> The varying shore o'the world!   (IV.xv.9-11)

Only Antony and Cleopatra dare to speak a hyperbolic, exaggerated poetry that envisions a 'new heaven, new earth' beyond 'The varying shore o' the world'. Their deaths are tragic, but the poetry they speak is life-affirming. They offer their audiences a bright world of possibilities.

4.4. IMAGES VISUALIZED ON STAGE

In a poetic drama like *Antony and Cleopatra*, imagery is not only verbal but also visual. What happens on stage will often make visually concrete a verbal image or, occasionally, contradict such an image and thus introduce unexpected ironies or tensions. In II.vii – the banqueting scene aboard Pompey's galley – the imagery of 'measure' associated with Rome is contradicted by the actual behaviour of the Romans. What we see in the theatre is a drunken revel that counters all talk of measure, balance, and propriety. Tensions are running high, and distrust and deceit are in the air; yet, at the same time, we have displayed before us the 'great fellows' of the Triumvirate, Pompey, and their followers joining hands in a loud, foot-stamping ring-dance while a boy sings a hymn to 'Plumpy Bacchus', the god of revelry (see Critical Commentary). The only one not drinking is Menas, the pirate, who hatches a plot to kill the triumvirs. Ironically, no such scene of hedonistic abandon takes place among the Egyptians although Romans are always accusing them of such behaviour. (Is that partly envy on the part of the Romans?) Even Antony and Cleopatra, whom the Romans accuse of the most sordid goings-on, have no intimate scene between them, and they are never alone together on the stage; we see them only in their public roles.

More often, however, the images that we see take their cue from what we hear. When her attendants dress Cleopatra in her robe and crown, we see clearly that she will not die as Antony's lover but as a great Queen. Charmian's setting straight the crown that has gone 'awry' after Cleopatra slumps down is a moving image that reflects the love that Cleopatra commands even after she is dead; Charmian sees to it that her mistress's death is in every way perfect. In III.xi, Antony '*sits down*' – a moving image of greatness humbled.

One of the recurrent images is that of Antony's sword – a symbol of both his heroic valour as a soldier and of his virility as a lover. (Agrippa observes that Cleopatra once 'made great Caesar lay his sword to bed. / He ploughed her and she cropped'. II.ii.228-9.) Cleopatra fondly reminisces about the time that she 'drunk' Antony 'to his bed; / Then put my tires [head-dresses] and mantles on him, whilst / I wore his sword Philippan' (II.v.21-3). Regarded by Caesar as 'womanly' (I.iv.7), Antony, in turn, mocks Caesar, who 'at Philippi kept / His sword e'en like a dancer' (III.xi.35-6), and later challenges him 'sword against sword' to determine who is the more manly (III.xiii.27) – a challenge that Caesar wisely turns down, much to Antony's surprise. Cleopatra wishes that 'Upon your sword / Sit laurel victory' as Antony sets out for Rome (I.iii.99-100), and later Antony swears that by his sword he 'will earn our chronicle' (III.xiii.175). After his first defeat at Actium , Antony tells Cleopatra that his love for her has made 'weak' his sword (III.xi.65-8); and, after his final defeat, thinking at first that she has betrayed him, he cries out, 'She has robbed me of my sword' (IV.xiv.23). Thus, the entrance of Decretas '*with the sword of Antony*', in the scene immediately following Antony's death startles Caesar (V.i.3-4), but the naked sword is a poignant reminder of all that remains of the fallen Antony in this world; his follower is using it to ingratiate himself with Caesar.

The hand, especially Cleopatra's, is another recurring image in both words and sight. Cleopatra boasts of her 'hand that kings / Have lipped, and trembled kissing' (II.v.29-30). Antony is driven almost to madness when he sees her offering her hand to Caesar's cunning ambassador Thidias (III.xiii.73-126); but, after his unexpected victory over Caesar later in the play, he commends his valiant, battle-scarred follower, Scarus, to Cleopatra and invites him to kiss her hand (IV.viii.22-4); a few lines later (29), he himself asks her to 'Give me thy hand' as they set out to march in triumph through Alexandria. Before he commits suicide, Antony envisions himself and Cleopatra walking 'hand in hand' in a world 'Where souls do couch on flowers' (IV.xiv.51).

One of the most fully realized images occurs in the monument scene (IV.xv). The effort by Cleopatra and her attendants in lifting Antony's heavy body, is, as 'ALL THE GUARDS' say, 'A heavy sight' (40). The phrase expresses both the pain of watching this scene of mortality and, simultaneously, the awe that the guards (and audience) are experiencing. Watching the three women lift Antony 'aloft' is to be made aware that something spiritual is going on: we see Antony being raised to a higher plane by the work of love. At this moment, the material and the spiritual, the human and the divine, come together. The image *taking place* before our eyes prepares us for the final transfiguration of the two lovers.

5 SPECIMEN PASSAGE AND COMMENTARY

Alarum. Enter ANTONY *again, in a march;* SCARUS, *with others*

ANTONY   We have beat him to his camp. Run one before
And let the Queen know of our gests. Tomorrow,
Before the sun shall see's, we'll spill the blood
That has today escaped. I thank you all,
For doughty-handed are you and have fought
Not as you served the cause, but as 't had been
Each man's like mine; you have shown all Hectors.
Enter the city, clip your wives, your friends,
Tell them your feats, whilst they with joyful tears
Wash the congealment from your wounds, and kiss   10
The honoured gashes whole.

Enter CLEOPATRA

[To SCARUS] Give me thy hand.
To this great fairy I'll commend thy acts,
Make her thanks bless thee. – O thou day o' the world,
Chain mine armed neck; leap thou, attire and all,
Through proof of harness to my heart, and there
Ride on the pants triumphing!

CLEOPATRA   Lord of lords!
O infinite virtue, com'st thou smiling from
The world's great snare uncaught?

ANTONY   My nightingale,
We have beat them to their beds. What, girl, though grey
Do something mingle with our younger brown, yet ha'we   20
A brain that nourishes our nerves, and can
Get goal for goal of youth. Behold this man,
Commend unto his lips thy favouring hand. –
Kiss it, my warrior. – He hath fought today
As if a god in hate of mankind had
Destroyed in such a shape.

CLEOPATRA I'll give thee, friend,
  An armour all of gold; it was a king's.
ANTONY He has deserved it, were it carbuncled
  Like holy Phoebus' car. Give me thy hand –
  Through Alexandria make a jolly march,   30
  Bear our hacked targets like the men that owe them.
  Had our great palace the capacity
  To camp this host, we all would sup together
  And drink carouses to the next day's fate,
  Which promises royal peril. Trumpeters,
  With brazen din blast you the city's ear;
  Make mingle with our rattling tabourines,
  That heaven and earth may strike their sounds together,
  Applauding our approach.

                                            [*Exeunt* IV.viii]

The scene begins with the noise of battle ('*Alarum*)' and ends with
the 'brazen din' of trumpets and the 'rattling' of drums ('tambouri-
nes') proclaiming a victory. This is the most stirring moment in the
play, and it falls at the halfway point of Act IV – an Act that began
with a defeated Antony perplexed by Caesar's refusal to fight a duel
with him (see IV.i,ii) and that will end with Antony's death in
Cleopatra's arms. Here, between defeat and death, Antony is caught
in a moment which finds him realizing to perfection his true self as
heroic in war and in love. In another happy scene (IV.iv) Cleopatra
had helped arm Antony for this battle and had watched him go 'forth
gallantly'. In the interim, Antony has fought as her 'soldier' and her
'servant' (see I.iii.70); and, defying all expectations, he has been
successful. For the lovers, this is their last fully joyous moment
together. For Antony, all that 'Rome' and 'Egypt' mean to him unite
here in harmony: his public and private aspirations co-exist without
stress. His first thought on returning from battle is of the 'Queen' (2);
the victory is hers as well. In images of military pride and sexual
pleasure he asks her to leap through his impenetrable armour ('proof
of harness') to 'ride' on his panting heartbeats (13-16), recalling
Cleopatra's earlier 'happy horse, to bear the weight of Antony!'
(I.v.21). Their love, like the 'proof of harness', has stood the test.
  Antony's mood recalls Cleopatra's characterisation of him – 'O
well-divided disposition!' (I.v.53): he neither dwells upon his victory
over Caesar nor brags about his own exploits, preferring to speak to
his soldiers of 'our gests' and 'your feats'. Antony's new found unity
of self is reflected in his simple, largely monosyllabic language: 'We
have beat him to his camp. Run one before / And let the Queen know
of our gests'. The simplicity of his 'I thank you all' (4) to his soldiers
attests its sincerity. There is real affection in the way that he greets

Cleopatra as 'My nightingale' in response to her magnificent welcome, but the affection seems even more genuine when he addresses her less lyrically as 'girl' (16-19): we had not witnessed this tenderness between them before. The Antony we now see is at peace with himself: no longer obsessed with the difference between Caesar's youth and his age, he jokes about his greying hair (19-22; compare III.xi.13-15); he recommends Scarus's hand twice to Cleopatra for a kiss (11-13, 22-4) whereas earlier he became enraged when he caught her extending her hand to Thidias (III.xiii.85 and following); he commends his men for having shown themselves 'all Hectors' (7), and he praises Scarus's valour (22-6) with no hint of that envy of which Ventidius had accused him (see III.i). In asking for Cleopatra's hand himself (29), Antony anticipates his later vision of himself and Cleopatra walking 'hand in hand' 'Where souls do couch on flowers' (IV.xiv.51). In contrast to 'this enchanting queen' from whom he felt he had to 'break off' (I.ii.129), Cleopatra is now a magical 'fairy', whose 'thanks' bestow blessings (12-13). Antony's call to the trumpeters to 'blast . . . the city's ear' so 'That heaven and earth may strike their sounds together, / Applauding our approach' (35-9) recalls his telling Cleopatra that only a 'new heaven, new earth' could set limits to their love (I.i.16-17). This is a moment of transcendence as he returns 'from / The world's great snare uncaught' (17-18), from death itself (as in Proverbs, 13:14, 'from the snares of death'). The phrase may even refer to Caesar, whose view of life's pleasures is a death force in the play. Antony has kept his promise to his followers to expect from him 'victorious life / Than death and honour' (IV.ii.42-4). Now he returns to the 'day o'the world' (13) – to the sun, to Cleopatra, the life force of the play; he relates the 'armour all of gold' that she has promised to Scarus to the jewel-encrusted chariot ('carbuncled . . . car') of the sun-god, 'holy Phoebus' (28-9), whom Cleopatra earlier had said made her 'black' with his 'amorous pinches' (I.v.28).

Although, historically, the play takes place in the early days of the Roman Empire, the language of the scene suggests medieval chivalry and pageantry. When he speaks of 'gests' (deeds, feats of valour; 2) and commends his 'doughty-handed' (valiant; 5) troops, Antony uses words that were, even in Shakespeare's day, old-fashioned. Soldiering is 'The royal occupation' (IV.iv.17) a profession that 'promises royal peril' (35). To him, his soldier's wounds are red badges of courage – 'The honoured gashes' made whole with kisses from wives and friends (9-11). Their 'hacked targets' or battered shields (31) are sources of pride. Antony speaks here mostly in monosyllables; and in this context the three-syllable word 'congealment' (10), the clotted blood from the wounds, is startling, but its formality and strangeness help to distance us from the actual horror of warfare: the 'gests' of Antony and his 'doughty-handed' knights are already passing into 'story' (III.xiii.46), into the formal context of art, where they will be forever celebrated.

This scene makes clear what the whole play implies: that the loyalty, feats of valour, and generosity that Antony regards so highly are values already becoming doomed in the Renaissance by the march of history. Antony's living by the sword contrasts with Caesar's behind-the-scenes calculations, as his generosity to his soldiers (he wishes that Cleopatra's 'great palace' [32] were large enough to hold his entire army) contrasts with Caesar's niggardliness (see IV.i). Even Cleopatra learns generosity from Antony and bestows 'a king's suit of 'armour all of gold' upon Scarus (26-7); later, after his death, she describes Antony's 'bounty' as having 'no winter in't – an autumn 'twas / That grew the more by reaping' (V.ii.86-8). For the medieval knight *courtoisie* – winning the love of a woman – animated the code by which he lived. Cleopatra is Antony's inspiration, and she rewards his triumph with genuine admiration: 'Lord of lords! / O infinite virtue' (from 'virtu' – manly courage). Earlier (I.v.72), she called him 'My man of men'; now in his triumph she calls him 'Lord'. Her words to Antony are like the music of the 'nightingale' he calls her (16-18). If the earlier comparison of Antony to a medieval knight made him appear foolish, here, even if the overtones are still ironic, it evokes a beautiful world recaptured, a remembrance of things past. But that world was rapidly receding from memory in Shakespeare's day, and the comparison also signals how fragile its recapture is. In Antony we see, in the words of Shakespeare's Sonnet 73, 'the twilight of such day / As after sunset fadeth in the west, / Which by and by black night doth take away'.

That 'sunset', however, is resplendent. By the end of the scene the stage is filled with colour (banners undoubtedly being unfurled), music, and excitement as Antony takes Cleopatra's hand and they lead Scarus and the other soldiers off to a victory march. Nevertheless, the brilliance of the moment seems inconclusive: Antony's victory has not determined the final outcome. Caesar has been driven back only to his camp. While Antony, as 'a child o' the time', is off to 'drink carouses to the next day's fate, / Which promises royal peril' (34-5), we can be sure that Caesar is in his tent plotting strategy to 'possess' the time (see II.vii.104-5). 'Tomorrow, / Before the sun shall see's', says Antony, 'we'll spill the blood / That has today escaped' (2-4) – a line with ironic forebodings of Antony's impending defeat. The next day's 'royal peril' will be perilous, we can suspect, to him, not to Caesar.

The exuberance of this scene might well make us uneasy. What are we, finally, to make of Antony here? Everyone in the audience knows, even before coming to the play, that Octavius Caesar will end up as Augustus Caesar, the sole ruler of the Roman Empire. Knowing the outcome of the story, are we to consider the Antony of this scene a braggart soldier? He calls his loyal followers 'all Hectors' (7); but Hector, who was ultimately defeated by Achilles, was a synonym in the Renaissance not only for a heroic warrior but also for a braggart. Or does the scene lead us to think of Antony as the noble flower of chivalry? The scene alone provides no absolute answer, but every scene in the play must be understood in the context of surrounding scenes (see 'Structure and Stagecraft'). After the 'brazen din' that ends the scene, the next begins in ominous silence. There, Enobarbus, who has chosen the ambitious, practical-minded Caesar and his world of reason over loyalty to Antony, dies broken-hearted from his choice. 'Antony' is the last word that he speaks. Enobarbus's strange death would seem to vindicate Antony.

6 STAGE HISTORY AND CRITICAL RECEPTION

There are no references at all to performances of *Antony and Cleopatra* in Shakespeare's day or during the entire seventeenth century. When in 1607 he revised his play of 1594, *Cleopatra*, Samuel Daniel added a passage that describes in very explicit theatrical terms how Cleopatra drew Antony up to her monument (IV.xv in Shakespeare) 'in rowles of taffety'. Daniel, we like to think, may have been describing what he saw in an actual performance of Shakespeare's play. Long before the seventeenth century was over, a 'Roman' judgement against the adulterous lovers prevailed; and, with the rise of neo-classicism in England after the Restoration in 1660, the sprawling structure of the play baffled those who looked for the classical unities of time, place, and action. In the 1677-8 season, John Dryden's version of the story, *All for Love; or, The World Well Lost*, appeared in the London stage. This version, in its structure and staging especially, was to exert an enormous influence, and passages from it found their way into several of the early nineteenth-century productions that returned to Shakespeare's by-now heavily edited text. Even in this century, Dryden's staging of Cleopatra's death, upright on her throne in a posture resembling Egyptian statuary rather than on a 'bed' as in Shakespeare, often ends the play.

In its own way *All for Love* might be considered a critical commentary on *Antony and Cleopatra*. Dryden claimed to have written his play 'in imitation of Shakespeare's style', but what he did essentially was to domesticize Shakespeare's most heroic play by replacing the grandeur of its highly metaphorical poetry with a much chastened rhetoric (though still in blank verse) and by confining the action to the last day of Antony's and Cleopatra's lives. The number of characters has been reduced, and all action takes place in one locale: the Temple of Isis at Alexandria. Instead of the overlapping scenes of Shakespeare's play, five chunky acts follow one another like a Newtonian law: the action of one act gives rise to an opposite reaction in the next. The whole conflict turns simply upon the opposition of love and honour. From the beginning, Antony is a 'ruin' of a man, and there is little or no complexity to Cleopatra: she loves as devoutly as any faithful wife, and she commits suicide very shortly after Antony does. Dryden writes for an actress in the role of Cleopatra, and the part has been considerably softened. Caesar never appears, and the political plot remains in the background.

Not until 1759 did Shakespeare's play return to the English stage, and then only in a heavily edited text by the famous actor David Garrick and his collaborator Edward Capell; this was the only production of the eighteenth century. Although Garrick and Capell did not interpolate passages from Dryden into their text, the Dryden influence operated in other ways: in the set blocks of action, the elimination or combination of characters, the cutting of most of the political scenes, and in the spectacle and scenery of the production. The Restoration stage of Dryden brought with it movable scenery; and by Garrick's time, the new, much larger theatres thrilled audiences with their visual splendour. By the nineteenth century, which saw several important revivals of the play (see Margaret Lamb, 'Antony and Cleopatra' on the English Stage, 1980, for details), spectacle and scene changes overwhelmed the text. It is almost a law for Shakespeare: the more scenery the less play. John Philip Kemble's production at Covent Garden in 1813 began a tradition that lasted to this century. Kemble was almost as much an antiquarian as an actor, and he placed great emphasis on the realism of Egyptian and Roman decor and costumes. Subsequent productions rivalled and outdid his attempts at verisimilitude; and they left nothing to the imagination, the use of which is, as we have seen, one of the play's prime themes.

Only after World War I was there a return to Jacobean modes of production with continuous performances that illuminated Shakespeare's structure and respected the full text. Simplified settings and Renaissance costuming were revived. Between the wars, the Old Vic and the Stratford Festival theatres took the lead in creating such productions. In the 'forties and 'fifties, London's West End witnessed three successful productions that emphasised the romance of the story. More recent productions have tended to lessen the appeal of the lovers or to be downright anti-romantic. Millions of viewers will continue to see the 1980 BBC production directed by Jonathan Miller; the small screen made more intimate the play of the lovers but at the same time reduced the scope of the larger play. Ideally, *Antony and Cleopatra* conveys a sense of both vastness and intimacy.

Theatrical productions have not kept pace with the wide-ranging literary and scholarly criticism of the play (see 'Further Reading' for suggestions). The major reassessment that began when Coleridge praised the 'happy valiancy' of its style and called it 'of all perhaps of Shakespeare's plays the most wonderful' continues today with an 'infinite variety' of approaches. Critics still tend to be either 'Romans' (who emphasise the realism and morality of the play) or 'Egyptians' (who emphasise its poetry and romance), but more and more the best critics transcend these categories. A student would be well advised not to rely on just one or two books or articles but rather to sample this variety and come to his or her own conclusions.

QUESTIONS

The purpose of the following questions is to help you explore *Antony and Cleopatra* in greater depth on your own. The best answers are those which refer constantly to *specific* details of character, action, and language. Impressions and feelings should be sustained by a hard look at the play itself.

1. Most readers and audiences of *Antony and Cleopatra* come to the play knowing that, historically, Octavius Caesar defeated Mark Antony in 31 B.C. to become sole ruler of the Roman Empire. Since we are likely to know the story in advance, how does Shakespeare build up dramatic suspense or tension?

2. The play has been described as having no heroes or villains. Do you think that this is a true assessment? Why?

3. Octavius Caesar is not a particularly likeable character, but he has the love of his sister and the respect of his followers; and he does fulfil his moment in history. Do you think that the play condemns him? or approves of him?

4. Examine all the many different ways that the various other characters view Antony and Cleopatra. Does any one viewpoint dominate? Consider, too, the different ways in which Antony and Cleopatra see themselves and each other from one scene to another.

5. The play has been called a 'tragedy', a 'tragi-comedy', and a 'divine comedy'. What would you call the play? And why? Do you find the ending satisfactory?

6. Early in the play, the Soothsayer says to Antony, 'If thou dost play with [Caesar] at any game, / Thou art sure to lose' (II.iii.26-7). In the light of this prophecy, would you consider *Antony and Cleopatra* mainly a play of character? or of fate? Why?

7. In his edition of *Shakespeare's Works* (1765), Samuel Johnson wrote, 'The events [in the play], of which the principals are

described according to history, are produced without any art of connection or care of disposition'. Take the opposite approach, and defend the plotting or structure (the 'art of connection') of the play.

8. Choose a fairly lengthy speech by Caesar and one by Cleopatra. Can you distinguish between a 'Roman' style and an 'Egyptian' style. How would you describe a characteristic speech by Antony?

9. Comment on Enobarbus as a 'choric' character, one who mediates between the characters in the play and us, readers or spectators. How far should we allow him to take us into his confidence?

10. The part of Cleopatra was written for a boy actor. Has this fact influenced Shakespeare in writing it? How so?

APPENDIX:

SHAKESPEARE'S THEATRE

We should speak, as Muriel Bradbrook reminds us, not of the Elizabethan stage but of Elizabethan stages. Plays of Shakespeare were acted on tour, in the halls of mansions, one at least in Gray's Inn, frequently at Court, and after 1609 at the Blackfriars, a small roofed theatre for those who could afford the price. But even after his Company acquired the Blackfriars, we know of no play of his not acted (unless, rather improbably, *Troilus* is an exception) for the general public at the Globe, or before 1599 at its predecessor, The Theatre, which, since the Globe was constructed from the same timbers, must have resembled it. Describing the Globe, we can claim therefore to be describing, in an acceptable sense, Shakespeare's theatre, the physical structure his plays were designed to fit. Even in the few probably written for a first performance elsewhere, adaptability to that structure would be in his mind.

For the facilities of the Globe we have evidence from the drawing of the Swan theatre (based on a sketch made by a visitor to London about 1596) which depicts the interior of another public theatre; the builder's contract for the Fortune theatre, which in certain respects (fortunately including the dimensions and position of the stage) was to copy the Globe; indications in the dramatic texts; comments, like Ben Jonson's on the throne let down from above by machinery; and eye-witness testimony to the number of spectators (in round figures, 3000) accommodated in the auditorium.

In communicating with the audience, the actor was most favourably placed. Soliloquising at the centre of the front of the great platform, he was at the mid-point of the theatre, with no one among the spectators more than sixty feet away from him. That platform-stage (Figs I and II) was the most important feature for performance at the Globe. It had the audience – standing in the yard (10) and seated in the galleries (9) – on three sides of it. It was 43 feet wide, and $27\frac{1}{2}$ feet from front to back. Raised ($5\frac{1}{2}$ feet) above the level of the yard, it had a trap-door (II.8) giving access to the space below it. The

SHAKESPEARE'S THEATRE

The stage and its adjuncts; the tiring-house; and the auditorium.

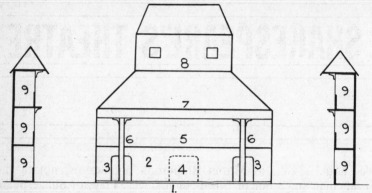

FIG I ELEVATION

1. Platform stage (approximately five feet above the ground) 2. Tiring-house
3. Tiring-house doors to stage 4. Conjectural third door 5. Tiring-house
gallery (balustrade and partitioning not shown) 6. Pillars supporting the
heavens 7. The heavens 8. The hut 9. The spectators' galleries

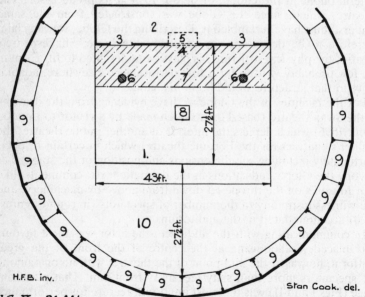

H.F.B. inv.

Stan Cook. del.

FIG II PLAN

1. Platform stage 2. Tiring-house 3. Tiring-house doors to stage
4. Conjectural third door 5. Conjectural discovery space (alternatively behind 3)
6. Pillars supporting the heavens 7. The heavens 8. Trap door 9. Spectators'
gallery 10. The yard

An artist's imaginative recreation of a typical Elizabethan theatre

actors, with their equipment, occupied the 'tiring house' (attiring house: 2) immediately at the back of the stage. The stage-direction 'within' means inside the tiring-house. Along its frontage, probably from the top of the second storey, juts out the canopy or 'Heavens', carried on two large pillars rising through the platform (6, 7) and sheltering the rear part of the stage, the rest of which, like the yard, was open to the sky. If the 'hut' (1.8) housing the machinery for descents, stood, as in the Swan drawing, above the 'Heavens', that covering must have had a trap-door, so that the descents could be made through it.

Descents are one illustration of the vertical dimension the dramatist could use to supplement the playing-area of the great platform. The other opportunities are provided by the tiring-house frontage or facade. About this facade the evidence is not so complete or clear as we should like, so that Fig. 1 is in part conjectural. Two doors giving entry to the platform there certainly were (3). A third (4) is probable but not certain. When curtained, a door, most probably this one, would furnish what must be termed a discovery-space (II.5), not an inner stage (on which action in any depth would have been out of sight for a significant part of the audience). Usually no more than two actors were revealed (exceptionally, three), who often then moved out on to the platform. An example of this is Ferdinand and Miranda in *The Tempest* 'discovered' at chess, then seen on the platform speaking with their fathers. Similarly the gallery (1.5) was not an upper stage. Its use was not limited to the actors: sometimes it functioned as 'lords' rooms' for favoured spectators, sometimes, perhaps, as a musicians' gallery. Frequently the whole gallery would not be needed for what took place aloft: a window-stage (as in the first balcony scene in *Romeo*, even perhaps in the second) would suffice. Most probably this would be a part (at one end) in the gallery itself; or just possibly, if the gallery did not (as it does in the Swan drawing) extend the whole width of the tiring-house, a window in the left or right-hand door. As the texts show, whatever was presented aloft, or in the discovery-space, was directly related to the action on the platform, so that at no time was there left, between the audience and the action of the drama, a great bare space of platform-stage. In relating Shakespeare's drama to the physical conditions of the theatre, the primacy of that platform is never to be forgotton.

Note: The present brief account owes most to C. Walter Hodges, *The Globe Restored*; Richard Hosley in *A New Companion to Shakespeare Studies*, and in *The Revels History of English Drama*; and to articles by Hosley and Richard Southern in *Shakespeare Survey*, 12, 1959, where full discussion can be found.

HAROLD BROOKS

FURTHER READING

Bibliography

T. J. B. Spencer, '*Julius Caesar* and *Antony and Cleopatra*', in
Shakespeare: Select Bibliographical Guides, ed. Stanley Wells
(Oxford University Press, 1973), pp. 203-15. A paperback, listing
important critical works and materials on sources and background.
With one or two exceptions, the following list is intended as a
supplement to it.

Collections of Extracts from Important Critical Works

John Russell Brown (ed.), *Shakespeare: 'Antony and Cleopatra', a
Casebook* (Macmillan Casebook Series, 1968). Includes generous
selections from, among others, A. C. Bradley on characterisation,
Harley Granville-Barker on the play's construction, and John
Middleton Murry and Maurice Charney on style and imagery.
Mark Rose (ed.), *Twentieth Century Interpretations of 'Antony and
Cleopatra', A Collection of Critical Essays* (Prentice-Hall, 1977).

Stage History and Critical Reception

Margaret Lamb, '*Antony and Cleopatra*' *on the English Stage* (Fair-
leigh Dickinson University Press, 1980).
Michael Scott, *Antony and Cleopatra* (Macmillan's Text and Performance Series, 1983, paperback). How the play is realised in
performance, including the 1980 BBC-Television production.

Recent Critical Works

Janet Adelman, *The Common Liar, An Essay on 'Antony and
Cleopatra'* (Yale University Press, 1973).
J. Leeds Barroll, *Shakespearean Tragedy: Genre, Tradition, and
Change in 'Antony and Cleopatra'* (Folger Books, 1984).

John Bayley, *Shakespeare and Tragedy* (Routledge and Kegan Paul, 1981). Chapter 5.

Barbara J. Bono, *Literary Transvaluation: From Vergilian Epic to Shakespearean Tragicomedy* (University of California Press, 1984). Chapter 4.

John Coates, 'The Choice of Hercules in *Antony and Cleopatra*', in *Shakespeare Survey 31* (Cambridge University Press, 1978), pp. 45–52.

Rosalie L. Colie, *Shakespeare's Living Art* (Princeton University Press, 1974). Chapter 4.

Michael Goldman, *Acting and Action in Shakespearean Tragedy* (Princeton University Press, 1985). Chapter 6.

Emrys Jones, *Scenic Form in Shakespeare* (Oxford University Press, 1971). Chapter 8.

Carol Thomas Neely, *Broken Nuptials in Shakespeare's Plays* (Yale University Press, 1985). Chapter 4.

J. L. Simmons, *Shakespeare's Pagan World: The Roman Tragedies* University Press of Virginia, 1973). Chapter 4.

Joseph H. Summers, *Dreams of Love and Power: On Shakespeare's Plays* (Oxford University Press, 1984). Chapter 6.

W. B. Worthen, 'The Weight of Antony: Staging 'Character' in *Antony and Cleopatra*', in *Studies in English Literature*, Vol. 26 (1986), pp. 295 – 308.